Yale Historical Publications
The Wallace Notestein Essays, 5

Published under the Direction of
the Department of History

JEFFERSON AND FRANCE

An Essay on Politics and Political Ideas

by

Lawrence S. Kaplan

NEW HAVEN AND LONDON
YALE UNIVERSITY PRESS
1967

Copyright © 1967 by Yale University.
Designed by Anne Rajotte,
set in Baskerville type,
and printed in the United States of America by
The Carl Purington Rollins Printing-Office
of the Yale University Press.
Distributed in Canada by McGill University Press.
All rights reserved. This book may not be
reproduced, in whole or in part, in any form
(except by reviewers for the public press),
without written permission from the publishers.

Library of Congress catalog card number: 67-13441

Published with assistance from the John Hay Whitney Fund

In Memory of My Father

Preface

Few qualities of Thomas Jefferson have been so noticed through the years as his attachment to France and everything French. Occasionally, it has won approbation. Vernon L. Parrington, for example, pointed out that the spirit of revolutionary France supported the program of social idealism that Jefferson put into effect as President.[1] On the other hand, Jefferson's enemies in every generation have traced most of his failures to the baleful influence of France. It is not surprising that his young contemporary, William Cullen Bryant, should have accepted his elders' judgments of Jefferson's Francophilism when in 1808 he identified him as "Napoleon's slave" and *"willing vassal* of imperious France."[2]

In the last two generations, there has been increasing recognition from scholars that Jefferson's philosophy was largely formed before he had visited France, and that if it had any special origins, Locke or Kames must receive credit or blame, not Rousseau or Condorcet.[3] Instead of a woolly minded dev-

1. Vernon L. Parrington, *Main Currents in American Thought: An Interpretation of American Literature, from the Beginnings to 1920* (3 vols. New York, 1927–30), 2, 10.

2. William Cullen Bryant, "The Embargo; or, Sketches of the Times: A Satire," *William Cullen Bryant: Representative Selections,* ed. Tremaine McDowell (New York, 1935), pp. 341 ff.

3. See for example: Gilbert Chinard, *Thomas Jefferson, Apostle of Americanism* (Boston, 1929); Charles M. Wiltse, *The Jeffersonian Tradition in American Democracy* (Chapel Hill, 1935); Dumas Malone, *Jefferson and the Rights of Man,* Vol. 2 of *Jefferson and His Time* (Boston, 1951); Merrill D. Peterson, *The Jefferson Image in the American Mind* (New York, 1960).

otee and enthusiast, the picture we now have of him is that of
a tolerant and somewhat patronizing teacher of the French,
encouraging them in their awkward groping toward democracy
but recognizing that their lack of experience with freedom and
responsibility would slow their advance. This is the Jefferson
who resented Napoleon's violence and deplored the excesses
of the French Revolution.

The friendly critic can even suggest without condescension
that Jefferson's thought was closely related to that of the French
idéologues—the liberal philosophers, scientists, and economists
who were subjected to vigorous criticism in the nineteenth
century.[4] His translations and support of the works of Destutt
de Tracy and of Jean Baptiste Say and his intimacy with Pierre
Samuel Du Pont de Nemours and with Lafayette all point to
strong links with the leading figures of the French intelligentsia.

What is less clear in this new evaluation of Jefferson is the
answer to the concomitant charge of his enemies: that his affini-
ties for France, Frenchmen, and French ideas led him, if unwittingly, into the services of the French Revolution and of
Napoleon. Particularly at the times of the undeclared naval war
with France in 1798, the embargo of 1807, and the War of 1812,
they claimed Jefferson pursued or urged policies which served
French interests. Did his attempts to exploit French sympathies
for America's advantage reflect a clear understanding of his
country's interests? Or was he the victim, dupe, or collaborator
of France's thrust for power in the era of the French Revolution
and Napoleon? It is worth examining the complex relationship
of Jefferson and France for the insights into his mind that the
examination may yield and for the light it may cast upon the
position of his young nation caught in the maelstrom of the
European conflict.

I have accumulated debts of many kinds over the years in
which I have been engaged on this project. I owe much to the
guidance of Professor Samuel Flagg Bemis who introduced me

4. Adrienne Koch, *The Philosophy of Thomas Jefferson* (New York,
1943), pp. 44–45.

to the theme in his seminar at Yale University in 1948. I am grateful for the grants given me by the American Council of Learned Societies in 1950–51 for a study of the influence of French political ideas upon Jefferson's foreign policy, and by the Alumni Development Fund of Kent State University from 1961 to 1963 for studies in the Age of Jefferson. The Institute of Early American History and Culture, through the *William and Mary Quarterly*, has provided a hearing for my views. Significant portions of Chapters 5, 6, and 7 have appeared in the April 1957 and July 1962 issues of that journal; I am happy to acknowledge its support. The final version of this essay has benefited from the careful editorial attention of Miss Dorothy M. Green of the Kent State University Library, in the typing of the manuscript. Belatedly, I wish to express my appreciation to my wife for the sleepless nights she spent fifteen years ago helping me complete the dissertation on which this book is based.

Contents

I.

Jefferson, France, and the American Revolution: 1743–1784

In an era when historians have been exploiting the behavioral sciences to answer historical problems, it seems reasonable to assume that "depth psychology" could link Thomas Jefferson with France at a very early age. A concept of the people and the nation logically preceded his firsthand experience of France. Given Jefferson's facility in the use of language as well as the extraordinary quantity of his writings, the historian might expect his letters, memoirs, or commonplace books to yield the kinds of information that permitted Freud to interpret the sources of Leonardo's genius or, more recently, William B. Willcox to explain the behavior of General Clinton in the American Revolution. The expectations are not realized.

Without denigrating the importance of the new tools or the insights cognate disciplines may provide, the student of Jefferson must question the meaning and relevance of France to Jefferson's early life. Evidence of any feeling in his youth about France or Frenchmen is too meager or too delphic to provide a useful link to his future relations with France. Attempts to evaluate a French influence in childhood or adolescence require a leap of faith incommensurate with the services supplied by the application of psychoanalytical principles. It is comforting to note that historian William L. Langer accompanied his plea for greater use of psychological doctrine with the observation that recent advances in psychoanalysis have made the experiences of earliest childhood less important for understanding later development than had been believed a generation ago.[1]

In Jefferson's formative years there was no particular awakening, either sudden or gradual, to the significance of France in his own life or in the life of his country. At the age of five he attended the school of a Scottish clergyman, William Douglas, from whom he learned a little French but not enough of anything else to warrant more than a line in his autobiography.[2] Something more might have emerged from his two years with the succeeding tutor, Reverend James Maury, who in addition to being a superior classical scholar was of French extraction. But if this son of Huguenots had transmitted any emotion about France it would not have been affection but fear of the French imperial menace, particularly during the French and Indian Wars.[3] If this hostility was passed on to his student, no record of it exists.

Yet France did have a role to play in the education Jefferson received under the tutelage of Maury and later of Professor William Small and his colleagues at the College of William and Mary. The young Virginian was nourished on the classical writings of Greece and Rome, and his mentors were all spokesmen for the rationalism of the age. That there was a connection between interest in classical antiquity and the rise of the Enlightenment is as apparent as the fact of a French contribution to its growth.[4]

It is more difficult to isolate a distinctive French component, as opposed to British, Italian or German. The dominant ideas of the educated elite on both sides of the Atlantic were international in character; if any one nation may be credited with

1. William L. Langer, "The Next Assignment," *American Historical Review, 63* (January, 1958), 288.

2. Alexander A. Lipscomb and Albert E. Bergh, eds., *The Writings of Thomas Jefferson* (20 vols. Washington, D.C., 1904), *1, 3*. Hereafter cited as L&B.

3. James Maury to James Fontaine, August 9, 1755, Ann Maury, *Memoirs of a Huguenot Family—from Autobiography of James Fontaine* (New York, 1853), p. 395.

4. Koch, *Philosophy of Jefferson*, p. 2.

leadership during Jefferson's formative years, it was England. Locke and Bolingbroke could speak of their English Revolution of 1688 which had raised the judgment of reason in government above that of common law and had applied the principles of natural law to protect the inalienable rights of the people. French or American disciples of the philosophy of the Enlightenment looked to England for guidance until the middle of the eighteenth century. But even if French writers had been preeminent earlier, France herself was a hated and feared enemy of this period. Whatever positive influence she was to exercise as a nation upon America had to wait until the cessation of hostilities had softened colonial animosities against everything French. By then Jefferson had completed his formative years.

The Peace of Paris in 1763 permitted a new French role in America. The image of a hostile and threatening France blurred at the very time that French writers were replacing English in influencing political thought. Jefferson's habit of copying quotations from the works of philosophers and moralists whom he admired in his student years has given posterity some idea of his thinking at this time. As for possible French influence upon his explorations one may point vaguely to the increased prestige of French thinkers in the 1760s and more specifically to the appearance of Frenchmen in his commentaries on political philosophers. Whether such references signify meaningful influence is another matter. It is more reasonable to conclude, as Gilbert Chinard does, that the *philosophes* and Jefferson drew from common sources: the ancient philosophers and such seventeenth-century English figures as Bolingbroke.[5]

As he recorded the words of moralists and poets in his *Literary Bible,* he also set down in his *Commonplace Book* quotations from his favorite political philosophers. The chief English exponents of the Enlightenment are all well represented, as are the leading Frenchmen, particularly Montesquieu, who is responsible for twenty-seven separate quotations in Jefferson's little book. Jefferson later renounced Montesquieu when the

5. Gilbert Chinard, ed., *The Literary Bible of Thomas Jefferson* (Baltimore, 1928), p. 34.

French Revolution made the latter appear to be primarily an exponent of conservatism and monarchy in republican eyes. Montesquieu, in other words, was equated with Great Britain in Jefferson's mind.[6]

A younger and less prejudiced Jefferson could see in Montesquieu's writings the concept of self-rule and the rationalization against interference of Parliament in the affairs of the colonies. The principle of the federal empire composed of equal states under the rule of a common king can be found in the extensive quotations from Montesquieu recorded in Jefferson's notes.[7] It is also worth noting the attention Jefferson gave to a passage which states that laws establishing the right of suffrage in a democratic government are fundamental, "because," he added in the margin, "by their votes the people exercise their sovereignty."[8]

Most of the quotations that Jefferson culled from Montesquieu and Helvétius are similar to those that he copied from earlier English writers, and for good reason. He and his countrymen were using them as impartial authority to give reasons for a course of action that was desirable for America after the Peace of Paris. They felt that their rights were being violated; like stricken men grasping at any help that might save them, they turned for support to French writers as freely as to English. The popularity of the former grew rapidly as the colonists perceived the service France could perform as a counterpoise to Britain.

What was developing from the studies of the young Virginian was an ideology compounded of the lessons of his own experience, of an attachment to the British tradition of individual rights, and of the teachings of British and French contributors to the Enlightenment. Jefferson expressed his political philosophy in the "Summary View" in 1774 more clearly than in any other document, including the Declaration of Independence.

6. Gilbert Chinard, ed., *The Commonplace Book of Thomas Jefferson* (Baltimore, 1926), p. 33.
7. Ibid., p. 269.
8. Ibid., p. 258.

The philosophy is neither English nor French nor classical; it is a distillation of exhaustive probings into the nature of society colored by his frontier environment and by pride in his Anglo-Saxon heritage and dressed in the language of the Enlightenment. He accepted the basic premises of every student of the Enlightenment and twisted them to his own ends. Exploiting the fact that all the writers, English and French alike, acknowledged the supremacy of natural law, he claimed that this law was being violated and that the colonists had a moral and legal right to take remedial action. The type of action to be taken would depend upon the needs of the individual situation.[9]

The transition from the "Summary View" to the Declaration of Independence was therefore not difficult for Jefferson. The Declaration merely changed the phraseology, added new British abuses, and substituted King for Parliament as villain.

With varying degrees of truth, authors have insisted that the Declaration owed its inspiration to Cardinal Bellarmine, Burlamaqui, Lord Kames, and even Thomas Paine.[10] It seems more satisfactory to accept Jefferson's own statement which his constitutionally feeble resistance to public criticism forced him to make in his old age:

> Neither aiming at originality of principles or sentiments, nor yet copied from any particular and previous writing, it was intended to be an expression of the American mind. All its authority rests then on the harmonizing sentiments of the day, whether expressed in conversation, in letters, printed essays, or the elementary books of public right, as Aristotle, Cicero, Locke, Sidney, etc.[11]

9. TJ, "A Summary View of the Rights of British America," in Julian P. Boyd, ed., *The Papers of Thomas Jefferson* (Princeton, 1950–   ), *1*, 121–35. Hereafter cited as Boyd.

10. Gaillard Hunt, "The Virginia Declaration of Rights and Cardinal Bellarmine," *Catholic Historical Review, 3* (October, 1917), 276–89; R. F. Harvey, *Jean Jacques Burlamaqui: A Liberal Tradition in American Constitutionalism* (Chapel Hill, 1937); for Lord Kames, Chinard, *Thomas Jefferson, Apostle of Americanism;* Joseph Lewis, *Thomas Paine, Author of the Declaration of Independence* (New York, 1947).

11. TJ to Henry Lee, May 8, 1825, L&B, *16*, 118–19.

Scholars have had difficulty in accepting Jefferson's explanation at face value. Although Carl Becker appears to have done so by observing that "where Jefferson got his ideas is less a question than where he could have got away from them," he then proceeds to give most of the credit to Locke.[12] If Jefferson saw fit merely to sandwich Locke in between Cicero and Sidney in the above quotation, Bernard Faÿ should be entitled to include Rousseau in Jefferson's "etc."[13]

Jefferson was using ideas that had no national stamp to solve a problem which he considered to be peculiarly American: that government was the business of the governed. Otis, Bland, Adams, and Mason—each in his own way—expressed the same sentiments, often more clearly but never more impressively than Jefferson. He and his colleagues never really abandoned their assumptions, and the assumptions never required continued connection with Britain for success. Their arguments may have been borrowed more from England than from France, because their language and culture stemmed from England, but philosophy as a lone weapon would never have seduced the colonies.

What turned America toward France for philosophic support was fundamentally a non-intellectual factor. It is well illustrated by the hope expressed in the "Declaration of the Causes and Necessity for Taking Up Arms," issued by the Continental Congress shortly after the Battle of Bunker Hill. Jefferson's chief opponent among his fellow authors was John Dickinson, who disliked Jefferson's draft for its denial—in the manner of the "Summary View"—of all parliamentary authority and its emphasis upon the establishment of a federal empire.[14] But conservative Dickinson agreed with radical Jefferson that British action had forced the colonies to take up arms, thereby

12. Carl Becker, *The Declaration of Independence: A Study in the History of Political Ideas* (New York, 1945), p. 27.

13. Bernard Faÿ, *The Revolutionary Spirit in France and America*, trans. R. Guthrie (New York, 1927), pp. 78–79.

14. TJ's draft of the "Declaration of the Causes and Necessity for Taking Up Arms," Boyd, *1*, 199–203.

initiating a course that would bring French thought as well as French arms to America. Dickinson wrote: "Our cause is just. Our union is perfect. Our preparations are nearly completed. Our internal resources are great; and our assurance of foreign assistance is certain."[15] Of all the reasons for confidence that Dickinson cites, the one which gives validity to the rest was the reference to the weight France could throw into the balance of power.

Jefferson realized no more than did his fellow countrymen at the outbreak of the war how important France would be to the winning of independence. The prospect of a friendly France did provide them with a hope for security but not with a sense of gratitude, for they assumed that the advantage they were giving to France by producing a rift in the British empire was fully as great as any help she might give them later in the war.[16] As one of the more important authors of the Revolution, Jefferson naturally shared these views. He revealed in letters written early in the war a confident expectation of French help for the American cause. There was almost a note of complacency in the following reference to France. In mentioning the tremendous supply problems that faced the unorganized colonies, he said: "As to the articles of salt, blankets &c. every colony I believe will be to shift for itself, as I see nothing but the measure of a foreign alliance which can promise a prospect of importing either, and for that measure several colonies, and some of them weighty, are not yet quite ripe. I hope ours is and that they will tell us so."[17] Whatever the difficulty, it would apparently be only temporary; the French alliance would settle it. Jefferson's appraisal of French support was ultimately correct, but not until his attitude toward France changed radically.

He had few doubts in the summer of 1776. Writing to his boyhood friend, John Page, from his vantage point in Phila-

15. John Dickinson's draft of the "Declaration of the Causes," ibid., *1*, 211.
16. Felix Gilbert, *To The Farewell Address: Ideas of Early American Foreign Policy* (Princeton, 1961), pp. 49–54.
17. TJ to John Page, May 17, 1776, Boyd, *1*, 294.

delphia, he observed with equanimity that "the French governor in chief of the W. Indies has not only refused to permit a
captain of a man of war to make prize of our vessels in their
ports but forbidden them to come within gun shot of the
ports."[18] Although this French action was certainly gratifying
to him, he considered it nothing that should not be expected of
a country so greatly benefited by the American Revolution. In
the same vein he accepted the service of individual Frenchmen
who wished to enlist in the fight against England. In fact, he
was not above advising the limitation of the military activities
of Frenchmen in America on grounds that were practical if
undiplomatic. Jefferson realized that too great an influx of
Frenchmen would create an unmanageable disciplinary problem and suggested that there were already enough French
gentlemen serving as volunteers. Because they did not bring
their own horses with them, they were aggravating the problem
of adequately supplying American cavalrymen.[19] Valid as these
arguments are, they show no gratitude for foreign help, no
realization of a need to propitiate the country from which the
volunteers came.

Jefferson's reasons for declining the opportunity to join the
diplomatic mission to France in 1776 were dictated by pressing
matters at home rather than by distaste for European travel.
The need to win France over to the American cause was still of
secondary importance to him, or he would have paid more
attention to the warning of Richard Henry Lee that everything
depended upon a successful mission to France.[20] Had Jefferson
taken Lee's words seriously, he would never have offered his
domestic cares as excuse for refusing the appointment, no matter
how devoted a husband and parent he might be.[21] In 1781 his
wife's illness was sufficiently serious to permit such an answer;
that was not the case in 1776.

Jefferson was far more interested in the constitution which

18. TJ to John Page, August 20, 1776, ibid., *1*, 498.
19. TJ to John Page, July 30, 1776, ibid., *1*, 482.
20. Richard Henry Lee to TJ, September 27, 1776, ibid., *1*, 522–23.
21. TJ to John Hancock, October 11, 1776, ibid., *1*, 524.

Virginia was then preparing than in a visit to France. Virginia in the transition from colony to state would, he realized, be ready to accept ideas that he had been pondering for years. He gave up the trip to France as well as a seat in the Continental Congress in Philadelphia in order to help form a new government at Williamsburg.[22] The opportunity to reform Virginia was to him the most important fruit of the Revolution, for Virginia in 1776, and not the United States, was his "country."[23]

Immersed in the affairs of his state, he seemed at this phase of the Revolution to have little time for a war being waged largely in the Middle Atlantic states. In vain did George Washington, commander of the Continental Army, appeal to Jefferson and to other prominent fellow-Virginians to come to Philadelphia and serve the country that needed them so badly. The three great Virginians of the day—Wythe, Mason, and Jefferson—had confined their activities to the state assembly.[24]

Formation of the French alliance with the United States marked the beginning of a change in Jefferson's opinion of France. All America hailed the new ally; Jefferson was not slow to express his personal gratitude. Revealing a sentiment previously lacking, he noted: "If there could ever have been a doubt before as to the event of the war, it is now totally removed by the interposition of France and the generous alliance she has entered into with us."[25] Upon the departure of Conrad Gérard, France's first minister to the United States, he took occasion to declare his "personal gratitude and affection" to the ally for her services to his country.[26]

The expression of personal gratitude was more than a term

22. L&B, *1*, 53.

23. Dumas Malone, *Jefferson the Virginian*, Vol. 1 of *Jefferson and His Time* (Boston, 1948), p. 379. TJ emphasized this view in his "Notes on Virginia."

24. Washington to Benjamin Harrison, December 18, 1778, in J. C. Fitzpatrick, ed., *The Writings of George Washington* (37 vols. Washington, D.C., 1931–40), *13*, 467.

25. TJ to Giovanni Fabbroni, June 8, 1778, Boyd, 2, 195.

26. TJ to D'Anmours, November 10, 1779, ibid., *3*, 173.

of courtesy in this case. As governor in 1780, he counted heavily upon the intervention of the French fleet to frustrate a British invasion of Virginia spearheaded by Benedict Arnold and reinforced by General Phillips. After a brief period of quiet early in his administration, he became increasingly disturbed by the growing number of British troops in Virginia. Against this force France appeared as a mighty host. Writing to General Gates in October 1780, as the storm was about to break over his head, he told of information he had received that the British were strung out from Newport News to the mouth of the Nansemond River, with the probable intention of coming up the James River. "Would it not be worth while to send out a swift boat from some of the inlets of Carolina to notify the French Admiral that his enemies are in a net if he has the leisure to close the mouth of it?"[27] Jefferson's faith in the ability of France to save the American cause, at least in his own state, was great. Repeated disappointments failed to weaken it. Three months later he wrote to Gates about a new opportunity to destroy the British in Virginia, this time by a French attack upon British shipping along the mouth of the James.[28]

The new French minister, La Luzerne, pressed by the Virginia delegates in Congress, made attempts to help Virginia to the extent of having Admiral Destouches sent from Newport, Rhode Island, with a few vessels.[29] At about the same time Washington was sending another Frenchman, Lafayette, with further help for Virginia. Governor Jefferson, of course, was overjoyed and, as usual in this period, he expressed his feelings of gratitude to the nearest French official in almost obsequious terms.[30]

French aid was at first a failure despite Jefferson's high hopes.

27. TJ to Horatio Gates, October 28, 1780, ibid., *4*, 78.
28. TJ to Horatio Gates, February 17, 1781, ibid., *4*, 637.
29. Theodorick Bland to TJ, February 9, 1781, ibid., *4*, 568; TJ to Steuben, February 19, 1781, ibid., *4*, 660. See also L. R. Gottschalk, *Lafayette and the Close of the American Revolution* (Chicago, 1942), p. 191.
30. TJ to Chevalier de Tilly, February 25, 1781, in Paul Leicester Ford, ed., *The Works of Thomas Jefferson* (12 vols. New York, 1904–05), *3*, 186–87. Hereafter cited as Ford.

Notwithstanding a brief visit of Destouches to Virginia waters, British troops under General Phillips seemed to have little trouble disembarking in Virginia to reinforce Arnold.[31] Jefferson was disappointed and expressed his disappointment, but not in the tone of recrimination he had used for the British.[32] He appreciated the help France offered him, however inadequate, and he made a special point of telling La Luzerne in his next application for aid just how greatly indebted the United States was to France.[33] Jefferson would not have exhibited any resentment so long as there was the prospect of further aid from France; when his letter is considered in context, however, it appears unlikely that he was being cynical in expressing these sentiments. Besides seeing France as America's arsenal for the immediate needs of the war and a prop for his own lowered morale in the dark days of 1781, he perceived in French aid an opportunity to secure for the United States economic as well as political independence of Britain.

Formal ending of the war did not greatly alter the fears and hopes Jefferson had contracted during hostilities. He still distrusted Britain; he still admired and needed France. There was the suspicion, shared by others, that Britain would never be reconciled to the loss of her colonies; would do everything in her power to take revenge upon the United States. They will wait, he thought, until our governments fail, and they will play upon our every weakness to destroy us; "from thence inculcates a useful lesson to cement the friendship we possess in Europe."[34] It was understood, of course, that the only true friend the United States had in Europe was France.

That Jefferson had lost his heart to France is not too surprising. Consider the extravagant praise that Washington be-

31. TJ to Col. Isaac Avery, March 21, 1781, Boyd, *5*, 193–94.
32. TJ to Samuel Huntington, March 28, 1781, ibid., *5*, 270.
33. TJ to La Luzerne, April 12, 1781, ibid., *5*, 421.
34. These ideas were Franklin's, but TJ considered them of sufficient importance to send them to Washington and to Virginia's Governor Benjamin Harrison. TJ to Washington, March 6, 1784, ibid., *7*, 15–16; TJ to Harrison, March 18, 1784, ibid., *7*, 42–43.

stowed upon the ally in the moment of victory: "The very important Share which our great Allies have taken in this Event, ought to endear them to every American, and their Assistance should be remembered with perpetual Gratitude."[35]

It might follow, then, that Jefferson would have joined those who denounced the suspicious John Jay and John Adams for signing conditional and preliminary articles of peace in 1782 without a final consultation with Vergennes, thus violating Congress' injunction that the envoys follow Vergennes' lead. His friend Madison certainly condemned those Congressmen who voiced suspicions of France's good faith, even though he would not go to the extreme of rebuking the commissioners for disobeying Congress. Jefferson was remarkably silent during the debate in Congress about the articles of peace. He said nothing to deplore the plenipotentiaries' behavior toward France or even to second Madison's mild statement about the anti-French sentiments implicit in the attitude of the American commissioners and their supporters in Congress. In the interest of immediate peace he unreservedly supported the final peace treaty.[36] This stand did not indicate suspicion of French motives or indifference to American obligations to France; it was dictated by Jefferson's policy of using France to further American interests—and American interests, in his mind, demanded immediate peace. Perhaps if Vergennes had objected more vigorously to the Anglo-American negotiation, Jefferson's reaction might have been different, but Vergennes accepted it and the bonds between the two allies were not broken.

Jefferson's reasons for wanting the negotiations with Britain concluded as quickly as possible despite possible French objections reveal an acute understanding of both the advantages and the liabilities the French alliance had for the United States. Without forgetting that France was a vital factor in the mainte-

35. Washington to TJ, November 30, 1781, ibid., 7, 134.
36. Journals of the Continental Congress, 26, 5, January 3, 1784. TJ was on the committee and wrote the report that wanted immediate ratification of the treaty by all the states.

nance of American independence, he did not neglect the equally important element of America's position in the general scale of nations. Absorbed as he was in domestic matters during this period, he sensed how France's European diplomacy might well work to the detriment of American fortunes. He realized that if Vergennes remained in power in 1783, that subtle statesman might embroil France in a new European war, perhaps over the Turkish Question, before peace negotiations on the disposition of America could be completed. The consequence of such a situation would be the stiffening of British peace terms, for a continental war would immobilize America's powerful ally. If only for this reason he advocated ratification of the peace with Great Britain.[37]

Notwithstanding France's distractions in Europe, she could still be useful to prevent America's reuniting with Britain. As a member of Congress in 1783 and 1784 Jefferson tried to keep the United States in a position to utilize the benefits France could provide. He spent much of his time urging the strengthening of the central government. He knew that French sympathy would evaporate rapidly unless the debts contracted during the war were paid. The Confederation itself could pay only as much as the states provided it, and there was no agency that could force the individual states to observe their obligations. He wanted Congress empowered to collect revenue from the states by tax, rather than by requisition, and to regulate commerce between the states and foreign nations. Only in that way could national credit be kept and the loans from France be paid off; only in that way could the United States be really accepted as an equal in the family of nations. If the Confederation failed to regulate commerce properly, jealousy among the several states would ruin trade with Europe and allow England to reassert her sovereignty once again. The government must have the power to use commerce as an instrument of diplomacy to

37. TJ to Harrison, December 17, 1783 ("Happy for us that we have got into port just as this storm is rising"), Boyd, *6*, 389; TJ to Harrison, December 24, 1783, ibid., *6*, 419.

retaliate against those countries which discriminated against American trade.[38]

Between the years 1776 and 1784 Jefferson had come to realize that a community of interest important enough to affect many of his ideas about domestic as well as foreign affairs existed between his country and France. His attachment to France rested for the most part on the practical advantages which close relations with France had given the United States, but there was in addition an important area of his attitude controlled by emotional factors, such as gratitude toward France and hatred for England. While the intensity of his emotions may not at this time have affected his judgment about France's usefulness to America, it did help to open a receptivity to French ideas as embodied in her culture, which had not been present in his formative years.

War provided Jefferson with opportunities for meeting Europeans who ordinarily would never have been to America, men carrying the stamp of French customs and manners. Soldiers like Lafayette, diplomats like the Chevalier d'Anmours, philosophers like the Marquis de Chastellux—all showed him a way of life that Jefferson had known about before only from books. He adapted himself happily to many customs ordinarily considered uncongenial to the average Anglo-Saxon and widely advertised as French, such as a delight in good food and wine, a taste for abstract philosophy, and a love of art and music. His pleasantest days during the war were spent in the company of cultivated prisoners of war, many of them Germans with a French education.[39]

Frenchmen were welcome everywhere in America after the alliance, for the entrance of France into the war seemed to be the logical culmination of that tentative friendship which had

38. TJ to Harrison, April 30, 1784, *ibid.*, 7, 139; TJ to Horatio Gates, May 7, 1784, ibid., 7, 225.

39. Marie Kimball, *Jefferson: War and Peace, 1776 to 1784* (New York, 1947), has an excellent chapter, "Europe Comes to Jefferson," on the friendships he made with foreigners, allies and enemies, in the first few years of the war.

its beginnings after the peace of 1763. The colleges quickly followed the salons in showing their appreciation of the French language. One of Jefferson's proudest boasts as governor was his introduction in 1779 of French into the curriculum of his alma mater, the College of William and Mary. The importance he attached to this act is seen in the prominence he gave it in his autobiography. While excluding most of the troubled events of 1779 to 1781, he emphasized the fact that he had changed the organization of that institution by abolishing the grammar school and the two professorships of Divinity and Oriental Languages and substituting a professorship of Modern Languages.[40]

It is not surprising, therefore, that the Marquis de Chastellux, traveling from New England to the South during the war, found so many new Francophiles, like one excessive enthusiast for all French fashions who wanted only the termination of "this little revolution" to effect a still greater one in the manners of the country.[41] Such adulation, however, could produce a touch of condescension if not contempt in the French visitor. The beauty of Jefferson's Monticello, on the other hand, filled Chastellux with wonder and admiration for the artistic taste of at least one American.[42]

Jefferson and Chastellux, like Jefferson and every Frenchman he met, took delight in each other.[43] The French found in him their American counterpart with virtues they lacked, a man of Continental culture who retained at the same time the qualities of the mythical noble savage. Jefferson's tribute to Chastellux might be applied to all his French friends: "No circumstance of a private nature could induce me to hasten over the several obstacles to my departure more unremittingly than the hope of having the Chevalr. de Chattlux [sic] as a companion in my

40. L&B, *1*, 74.
41. François Jean, marquis de Chastellux, *Travels in North America, in the Years 1780, 1781, and 1782*, ed. H. C. Rice, Jr., ed. (2 vols. Chapel Hill, 1963), *1*, 135.
42. Ibid., 2, 390–91.
43. Ibid., 2, 392. He told here of the pleasure both received from reading together the poems of Ossian.

voiage. A previous acquaintance with his worth and abilities had impressed me with an affection for him which under the then prospect of never seeing him again was perhaps imprudent."[44]

These warm sentiments bestowed on a man whom Jefferson had known for only a very brief time were distributed in equal abundance to other French acquaintances. The most striking example was the relationship between Jefferson and Lafayette begun in the midst of the British invasion of Virginia. Despite the constant danger of friction brought on by a difficult military situation, they treated each other with courtesy and consideration. Not once did the dashing young general allude to France's great service to the American cause; not once did he try to criticize Jefferson's way of running the war in Virginia. Instead, he displayed a properly eager desire to meet the author of the Declaration of Independence and deplored the inability of the French fleet to give Virginia more support in 1781.[45] Jefferson was more than willing to meet him halfway. He was somewhat ashamed of the poor impression his state must have presented to this representative of powerful France and hence all the more grateful for whatever aid she chose to give the United States.[46] Out of these brief encounters began a lifelong friendship.

The increasing attraction of France and of Frenchmen was also responsible for the reversal Jefferson made in his attitude toward the various opportunities he had to visit Europe. In 1776 he had been apathetic about the prospect, being far more interested at the time in advancing his projects in Virginia than in visiting the seat of culture.[47] When Congress again offered him a chance to join the peace mission to Europe in the summer of 1781, Jefferson again declined but for very different reasons. He had to remain in Virginia to watch over his sick

44. TJ to Madison, November 26, 1782, Boyd, *6*, 207.
45. Lafayette to TJ, February 21, 1781, ibid., *4*, 676; Lafayette to TJ, March 16, 1781, ibid., *5*, 159–60.
46. TJ to Lafayette, March 2, 1781, ibid., *5*, 43; TJ to Lafayette, March 12 [1781], ibid., *5*, 130.
47. TJ explained his reasons in the *Autobiography* (L&B, *1*, 75–76).

wife and to defend himself against the attacks being leveled
upon his administration as governor. This time he was keenly
aware of what he was passing up: "an opportunity, the only one
I ever had and perhaps ever shall have of combining public
service with private gratification, of seeing count[ries] whose
improvement in science, in arts, and in civilization it has been
my fortune to [ad]mire at a distance but never to see."[48] After
a third invitation, received after the death of his wife and his
exoneration in Virginia, he was at last ready and able to go to
France.

48. TJ to Lafayette, August 4, 1781, Boyd, *6*, 112. He explained this situation more fully in a letter to Edmund Randolph, September 16, 1781 (ibid.,
6, 117–18).

2.

The Revolutionary as Diplomatist: 1784–1789

The terms "Old World" and "New World" connote the roles of master and pupil respectively, and it is the rare American even today who is not conscious of the fact that he has come upon a civilization which has given birth to his own. Consequently he is uneasy in the presence of Europeans, feeling a sense of inferiority expressed less by self-abasement before the age and dignity of his hosts than by an exaggerated contempt or indifference for their culture. If such can be the reaction of Americans to Europe in the century of America's power, the insecurity of former colonials in eighteenth-century Europe is readily understandable.

As proud of America as Jefferson was, he could not avoid displaying on occasion some of the traits of an innocent abroad as he made that long-promised journey to Europe in 1784. No matter how much he enjoyed the social life of the *Ancien Régime* he was unable to surrender his puritanical suspicion of corruption at the core of French culture, exemplified particularly by the role of women in society. The sight of them speaking out as equals in the company of men shocked him into an appreciation of the American homemaker whose simple virtues emphasized the artificiality of French mores. A constant refrain in his correspondence was the contrast between the healthy habits of America and the unnatural customs of France. On those occasions he would project himself back into the image of the frontiersman, almost the noble savage of Rousseau's dream, playing contentedly in his wild hills and living a far happier life than the overcivilized Parisian. Despite the implication of American superiority in this attitude, some of his protests sounded as if he were trying to compensate for his own uneasiness among his sophisticated associates.

The very evils against which he warned his friends exercised a great fascination upon him. In more relaxed moments he would admit his enjoyment of French life—the classical architecture, the intellectual atmosphere, not to overlook the native hospitality and French cooking. His colleague, Benjamin Franklin, introduced him almost immediately to the best society of France, complete with wicked women and effete men. The attraction was mutual, and an important factor in submerging any conceivable sense of inferiority was undoubtedly the homage of philosophers, statesmen, and scientists who knew him as the author of the American Declaration of Independence. The knowledge of being a veteran among the neophyte reformers of France outweighed any bashfulness he may have felt about being an American in Europe. Next to America, France was his favorite country.

Jefferson was in France as a diplomatist for his young nation, not as a political reformer or a man of culture indulging private tastes. The responsibilities of his duties governed his behavior abroad. Dispatched by the Confederation to France to join Adams and Franklin in establishing commercial treaties with European powers, he succeeded Franklin upon the latter's retirement as Minister to France. He conscientiously made all his social activities serve the needs of America's foreign policy. Those needs were the corollary of two axioms which Jefferson conceived to be keys to America's position in the balance of power: first, the existence of British power as a permanent threat to his nation's security through its economic if not military control over the United States; second, the position of France as a potential counterweight to Britain. From these two assumptions flowed most of his subsequent thought and actions connected with France.

Jefferson's policy was to use the negotiation of commercial

treaties to combat Britain's economic domination of the United States. If he could break down the trade barriers which shut out American products from Europe, Americans would be able to break their habit of dealing exclusively with Britain. "I would say, then, to every nation on earth, *by treaty,* your people shall trade freely with us, and ours with you, paying no more than the most favoured nation."[1] Realizing that the ideal of free trade was impossible to achieve, Jefferson was willing to accept the alternative that each country pay to the other only such duties as would the nations most favored in this respect. This plan would free the United States from special discrimination, at least, and perhaps open the way for additional privileges in the future. Although not specifically mentioned in these observations, France was the one country that could best serve the United States.[2] Jefferson's purpose was not preferential status for France as an ideal in itself; only France could perform the twofold function of replacing Britain in the economic life of the United States and of protecting America from British military designs.[3]

Dependent upon the good will of influential Frenchmen for the execution of his plans, and susceptible to the charm of their personalities, Jefferson could easily have come under the spell of men and ideas. His circle of friends included for the most part passionate admirers of America, liberal aristocrats and middle-class reformers who had lionized Franklin.[4] Few were republicans and even fewer were democrats. All hoped to give France a more satisfactory system of government which would

1. TJ to James Monroe, June 17, 1785, Boyd, *8,* 231.
2. TJ to Monroe, June 17, 1785, ibid., *8,* 232.
3. TJ to Lucy Ludwell Paradise, August 27, 1786, ibid., *10,* 304–05. See Merrill D. Peterson, "Thomas Jefferson and Commercial Policy, 1783–1793," *William and Mary Quarterly,* Third Series, 22 (1965), 592.
4. Marie Kimball, *Jefferson: The Scene of Europe, 1786 to 1789* (New York, 1950), pp. 82 ff.; Gilbert Chinard, *Jefferson et les idéologues, d'après sa correspondance inédite avec Destutt de Tracy, Cabanis, J.-B. Say, et Auguste Comte* (Baltimore & Paris, 1925), p. 5; Durand Echeverria, *Mirage in the West: A History of the French Image of American Society in 1815* (Princeton, 1957), p. 51.

secure for the French the happiness, if not all the freedom, of the liberated Americans. They were philosophers and spinners of political systems, with whom Jefferson enjoyed a free exchange of ideas and an appreciation of the refinements of civilized society. The common denominator of all his friendships in France was good will toward America. Whatever influence they exercised upon Jefferson's judgment at this time must be measured against the advantage they gave to his country.

He was always eager to send ideas of his French friends along to his American correspondents. Their conversation stimulated him; but his enthusiasm for the ideas of Frenchmen seemed restricted to philosophical methods and philosophical positions which agreed with his own preconceptions.[5] His association with the physiocrats showed how he applied new ideas to his American frame of reference while accepting only as much of the foreign doctrine as his earlier experiences confirmed. Physiocracy itself was part of the general revulsion from mercantilism, as best expressed by Adam Smith in England. Like other intellectual phenomena of the eighteenth century, physiocracy appealed to natural law for its rationalizations. Under the leadership of Quesnay and the elder Mirabeau, the physiocrats devised a system of society in which all moral as well as economic values rested on land and agriculture.

There was much in physiocracy which Jefferson approved— veneration of the farmer, dislike of excessive government interference in economic activity—but his chief bond with the physiocrats was their admiration for the United States. In most respects their ideals and ambitions were different from his. Essentially they were dogmatic in their philosophy while he was a pragmatist.[6] Jefferson's judgment was colored by his conception of his country's needs; he might approve the efforts of the

5. Koch (*Philosophy of Jefferson*, p. 73) emphasized his interest in the methodology of ideology. TJ's objections to Tracy's preoccupation with metaphysics are expressed in his letter to Duane, April 3, 1813, in Chinard, *Jefferson et les idéologues*, pp. 111–12.

6. TJ to Madison, January 12, 1789, Boyd, *14*, 437, for TJ's opinions of physiocrats as doctrinaires.

physiocrats in fighting the tobacco monopolists while looking askance at the low-tariff Anglo-French treaty of 1786 even though the latter conformed with physiocratic principles. Even identification of Jefferson with physiocrats through common interest in advancement of the farmer is fallacious. They were not speaking of the same "farmer." The French dreamed of the aristocratic values inherent in the noble's estate; Jefferson measured the small farm and farmer in terms of democratic values.[7]

It is as difficult to make Jefferson into a consistent philosopher of agrarianism as a physiocrat. Awareness of the frailties of the infant republic and of human nature had modified his concept of agrarianism long before the demands of the Presidency affected his policies. It is true that some of the most stirring passages in Jefferson's writings are eulogies of farmers, living as the "chosen people" on the fruit of their own industry, untouched by the corruption of commercial life.[8] Such sentiments are expressed in his correspondence and particularly in his "Notes on Virginia." But they were for the most part mere outbursts inspired by fear of Britain, and at best they represented vague hopes rather than guides for action. Believing that a self-sufficient agrarian economy would automatically save the country from the clutches of British merchants, Jefferson understood even better than the British the extent to which Americans were attached by habit to commerce. His aim was to make a virtue out of a necessity by accepting the permanence of a commercial economy and facilitating the transfer of commerce from Britain to France.[9]

It is unfortunate that the most sensational of his statements about commerce has been usually abstracted from the body of the text without the inclusion of important modifications. When he exclaimed that he wanted America to abandon com-

7. A. Whitney Griswold, *Farming and Democracy* (New York, 1948), pp. 29–31.

8. TJ to John Jay, August 23, 1785, Boyd, *8*, 426–27; TJ to G. K. van Hogendorp, October 13, 1785, ibid., *8*, 633. See also his "Notes on Virginia," L&B, 2, 229.

9. TJ, "Notes on Virginia," ibid., 2, 240–41.

merce and navigation and to "stand, with respect to Europe, precisely on the footing of China," he admitted freely that he was only indulging in a theory, "and a theory which the servants of America are not at liberty to follow. Our people have a decided taste for navigation and commerce . . . and their servants are in duty bound to calculate all their measures on this datum."[10] His allusion to China, furthermore, must be regarded as fanciful. China, like the Persia of Montesquieu, was strange enough and distant enough to point up through its imaginary virtues the shortcomings of his own country. Monroe had used the same theme of Chinese isolation only four months earlier in a letter that reached Jefferson before he himself used it.[11]

The difficulty in identifying Jefferson with any particular philosophic group is in finding a philosophic mold in which his ideas will fit. He was a politician and a statesman during most of his active life, before he was a philosopher, and the responsibilities of public duties with their emphasis on expediency served to strengthen his reluctance to accept the implications of formalistic thought.

The fact that Jefferson found no doctrines or masters in France to which or to whom he might attach himself did not indicate any indifference on his part to the ideas and men that circulated around him. He was constantly aware that the United States had to depend upon the favor of men of influence for any political and economic aid that France would give the United States. America, in the minds of Lafayette and Du Pont, had achieved the dreams of the French philosophers of the last generation. If they were to press America's cause at the Court of Versailles, they had to be assured that America's virtues had not been tarnished by success; that America itself was still worthy of their support. Jefferson took a justifiable pride in handling this task. He could cite his own personal accomplishments, such as the framing of Virginia's Statutes of Religious Freedom, as examples of America's loyalty to the principles of

10. TJ to G. K. van Hogendorp, October 13, 1785, Boyd, *8*, 633.
11. Monroe to TJ, June 16, 1785, ibid., *8*, 216.

freedom.[12] On the same note of pride he publicized other American institutions to which Frenchmen might look with envy: a representative system of government, absence of a hereditary aristocracy, equality of opportunity for all.

There were, however, serious problems in the United States that detracted from Jefferson's presentation of America's achievements. His European friends saw the negative as well as the positive features of the new republic. Economic dislocation and social unrest which followed in the wake of the Revolution tempered the examples of progress he had so proudly cited. The government of the Confederation lacked the necessary powers to cope with the management of thirteen autonomous states. The result of its structural weakness was the possibility that democratic rebellion on the one hand and monarchical reaction on the other would destroy the fruits of the Revolution. Jefferson understood this situation, but fearful of alienating America's liberal supporters in Europe, hesitated between favoring a movement for stronger central government that might provoke the charge of betrayal from the doctrinaire reformers, and advocating the continuation of a powerless government that only invited chaos at home and contempt abroad.

Jefferson's reaction to incipient civil war in Massachusetts revealed the conflict he saw between America's need to promote an image of stability in order to establish financial credit in Europe and her equally great need to demonstrate that in the New World the European example of curtailing the liberties of citizens would not be followed. He regarded Shays' Rebellion with mixed feelings, calling the rebels malcontents and recognizing the dangers awaiting American institutions at the hands of mobs and demagogues, yet understanding the farmers' reasons for rebellion.[13]

These rational observations were directly affected by the course of events in France which impelled Jefferson to assume an increasingly benign attitude toward the rebels, with a corresponding loss of respect for the forces of law and order. As

12. TJ to Mirabeau, August 21, 1786, Boyd, *10*, 283.
13. TJ to William Carmichael, December 26, 1786, ibid., *10*, 633.

the French turned to the reform of their government in 1787, Jefferson sensed the new importance of the American example in this reformation and felt that American prestige among the reformers would suffer seriously from stories of despotism in any form in America at the very moment they were themselves taking action against despotism in France. His earlier warnings against executive weakness changed into warnings against monarchy and reaction; his language became more extravagant as the tempo of the incipient French revolution mounted. He asserted that "the spirit of resistance to government is so valuable on certain occasions, that I wish it to be kept always alive," and professed uneasiness because there had been only one rebellion in the thirteen states since the American Revolution. According to his figures, France had enjoyed three insurrections in the three short years he had been in that country![14]

Jefferson's friends, further removed from the exciting events in France, did not share his fear for the future of American republicanism. On the contrary, John Adams, American Minister to England, whose opinions on foreign affairs had usually coincided with Jefferson's, fulminated—in the words of his wife Abigail—against "desperadoes, without conscience or principals [sic]," and warned darkly against demagogues who deluded the people.[15] Madison and Washington were equally severe in condemning Shays' Rebellion: for Madison the rebellion was not a glorious demonstration of man's love of freedom but a symptom of the government's inability to cope with anarchical forces.[16]

Jefferson's distance from events in America, combined with his sensitivity to events in France, produced a new attitude toward the strengthening of the central government. In his first years in France, he had shared the position of the framers of

14. TJ to Abigail Adams, February 22, 1787, ibid., *11*, 174; TJ to William Stephens Smith, November 13, 1787, ibid., *12*, 356; TJ to Madison, December 20, 1787, ibid., *12*, 442.

15. Abigail Adams to TJ, January 29, 1787, ibid., *11*, 86.

16. Madison to TJ, March 19, 1787, ibid., *11*, 220–21; Madison to Edward Pendleton, April 22, 1787, in Gaillard Hunt, ed., *Writings of James Madison* (9 vols., New York, 1900–10), *2*, 354–55.

the Constitution: fear of anarchy and desire to clothe the government with more powers. He voiced these needs in his diplomatic capacity.[17] And yet his first reaction to news of the Constitutional Convention was to condemn the absence of any guarantees of individual rights in the proceedings and to deplore the dangerous powers given to the executive office of the proposed government. These unpleasant features made him wonder whether it would not have been better to have merely added a few essential articles "to the good, old and venerable fabric," and not run the risk of losing liberty in the search for a stronger government. At best he considered himself a neutral in the matter of its adoption.[18] It is a credit to Jefferson's judgment that the pressure in France did not force him into an irreconcilably extreme position at this time. He ultimately accepted the Constitution, after he had been assured that the necessary safeguards would be provided as soon as the new government was inaugurated.[19]

Behind his objections to the handling of Shays' Rebellion and his misgivings about the Constitution lay his concern for the effect upon the blossoming French Revolution of America's putative fall from republican grace. Americans might have lost some of their fear of monarchy after their successful revolution, but would French reformers understand why his fellow countrymen no longer considered an increase in the power of the executive to be a threat to republicanism? Jefferson felt that Frenchmen would be skeptical of America's rationalizations, and he showed his sympathy for their doubts by telling his American correspondents that they would never underestimate the powers of monarchy if they ever witnessed its evils in Europe.[20] The

17. TJ wanted the states to be "made one as to all foreign, and several as to all domestic matters." TJ to Joseph Jones, August 14, 1787, Boyd, *12*, 34.

18. TJ to John Adams, November 13, 1787, ibid., *12*, 351.

19. For a time TJ was unwittingly involved in state politics. Opponents of the Constitution used his reservations to denounce the document and forced the friends of the Constitution to appeal to him for clarification of his views. See, for example, Madison to TJ, July 24, 1788, ibid., *13*, 412–13.

20. TJ to Monroe, August 9, 1788, ibid., *13*, 490; TJ to Benjamin Hawkins, August 4, 1787, ibid., *11*, 684.

Bill of Rights therefore signified something far more important than protection of Americans from the abuses of the federal government, for its absence would disappoint the "enlightened part of Europe," the men now coming to power in France who gave the United States credit "for inventing this instrument of security for the rights of the people, and have been not a little surprised to see us so soon give it up."[21] Jefferson's attitude toward constitutional developments in America was the product in part of a variety of factors related to France—solicitude for his personal prestige among the French, anxiety for American republican institutions accentuated by his immersion in French troubles, and consideration of American advantage to accrue from a friendly French regime.

There is a strong temptation induced by Jefferson's observations on the nature of society and government to regard his ideas as applicable to any time and place. According to John Locke, when the contract subsisting between ruler and people is violated the people have the right to assert their sovereignty by appealing to the natural law of rebellion. That contract was broken in America, by the British king; it was broken also in France, by the French nobility. An identification between the two situations is easily established and Jefferson apparently did not contradict it. When he spoke privately of rebellion as a positive good he did not restrict its benefits to the United States; he pointedly mentioned France.[22] When he urged Americans to preserve their liberties, his expression of fear of French censure for any American lapse suggested that the French were the equals of Americans in the knowledge of liberty and could complete successfully a revolution similar to theirs.[23] If this summary of Jefferson's position is valid, he was indeed a devotee of the French Revolution.

Notwithstanding his fulminations over the right of rebellion,

21. TJ to Francis Hopkinson, March 13, 1789, ibid., *14*, 650–51.
22. TJ to Madison, December 20, 1787, ibid., *12*, 442. See also TJ to William Stephens Smith, November 13, 1787, ibid., *13*, 356.
23. TJ to Edward Carrington, January 16, 1787, ibid., *11*, 48–49.

his understanding of Locke's ideas was based on America's enjoyment of a common heritage with England. He had always assumed in his writings and public speeches that Americans possessed the rights of British subjects—rights which had been betrayed by the British Parliament.[24] The rights for which the colonials fought were parochial rather than universal, the result of a peculiar experience in the New World and a peculiar heritage from the Old World. It is doubtful that Jefferson believed that the goals of the American Revolution could be won by Frenchmen, Germans, or Russians. Those people lacked the historical background and institutions of self-government: the tradition of free speech, the right of *habeas corpus,* the practice of suffrage. Only in the Declaration of Independence did Jefferson clearly state these rights in universal terms, and then the purpose was specifically to justify American action to the world, not to outline a program of world revolution.[25]

The American Minister's appreciation of the differences in the political environments of France and America was fortified by a tour of southern France in 1787. The people, he noted in his travels, had little in common with American yeomen; they were so incredibly poverty-stricken that he was moved to observe: "Of twenty millions of people supposed to be in France I am of opinion there are nineteen millions more wretched, more accursed in every circumstance of human existence, than the most conspicuously wretched individual of the whole United States."[26] The ignorance and passivity of the peasants which facilitated their exploitation by their government and their landlords were almost incomprehensible to him.[27] Here was no material for self-government. Granted that his disgust was primarily for the government of the *Ancien Régime,* it must

24. The "Summary View" of 1774 in particular emphasized this assumption.
25. Becker, *The Declaration of Independence,* pp. 20–23.
26. TJ to Eliza House Trist, August 18, 1785, Boyd, *8,* 404.
27. "Memorandums Taken on a Journey from Paris into the Southern Parts of France and Northern of Italy, in the Year 1787," ibid., *11,* 415–62. His observations reflected distaste as well as shock over the poverty and ignorance he found on this tour.

necessarily have extended to people who would permit themselves to be so misgoverned. Not only are the French not the free-minded people we in America think they are, he informed George Wythe, but it would take them a thousand years to achieve America's political accomplishments.[28]

Even the intelligentsia did not escape this judgment, despite Jefferson's reliance upon their connections at Versailles. The idealization of America in the writings of Brissot and Crèvecoeur disturbed as well as flattered him; he knew well that reality would never satisfy those Frenchmen nurtured on a Utopian myth. Two of his disciples precipitated an embarrassing controversy over the question whether Chastellux had slurred the United States by accusing the Quakers of indifference to the public welfare in their behavior during the American Revolution; Chastellux's comments suggested, furthermore, that Americans in general were somewhat less than perfect.[29] Jefferson was thereby placed in the uncomfortable position of knowing that Chastellux's account of American life was too mild rather than too harsh, and yet of being unable to express this idea to the aroused opponent Brissot. He tried to temper subtly some of the enthusiasm he had generated in France by declining Brissot's invitation to join his abolitionist society and by privately urging other friends making the journey to America not to expect too much from the New World.[30] He had learned from his French experience that although admiration in France for America might be sincere, it would be shallow if not based upon a true understanding. France and her Revolution may have lessened Jefferson's objectivity in interpreting the course of America's development during his absence from home, but his experience as an American prevented his confusing the American Revolution with the French Revolution.

28. TJ to George Wythe, August 13, 1786, ibid., *10*, 245.

29. Eloise Ellery, *Brissot de Warville: A Study in the History of the French Revolution* (Boston, 1915), pp. 59–60; *Mémoires de l'abbé Morellet*, ed. M. Lemontey (2 vols. Paris, 1821), *1*, 313.

30. TJ to Brissot de Warville, February 11, 1788, Boyd, *12*, 577–78; TJ to Madame de Brehan, October 9, 1787, ibid., *12*, 222; TJ to Moustier, October 9, 1787, ibid., *12*, 225.

With all his talk about the right of rebellion, he did not intend to accept Frenchmen as the political equals of Americans.

What gave impetus to his endorsement of the French Revolution was the failure of all but the most superficial part of his diplomacy in France. Yet on paper his success was remarkable. With the enthusiastic support of friends of America, Anglophobes, and physiocrats he induced the French government to remove many obstacles to American commerce. Prohibition of import duties on whale oil was lifted for American oil as a direct result of his pleas to that end. He even managed to break the monopoly Robert Morris had enjoyed in tobacco through his exclusive three-year contract with the Farmers-General. But all these victories were ephemeral. Even as France was opening her markets to American products, American profits from the tobacco and oil trade were immediately consumed in the purchase of accustomed British manufactures, rather than used to expand American markets for French industry. Such behavior only confirmed the suspicions of a French bourgeoisie which was too inefficient and custom-bound to understand and profit from Jefferson's or Vergennes' or the physiocrats' conception of Franco-American commercial relations.[31]

The basic obstacle in Jefferson's path was the politico-economic structure of France: a mercantilist monarchy with imperialistic ambitions. Under certain circumstances an autocratic government wisely pursuing its interest in foreign affairs could be of great service to a country like the United States, as French intervention in 1778 proved. These circumstances were no longer present in France. The American Revolution seemed to have drained the last bit of energy from her political system. Nothing remained but the shell of the Sun King's former strength, and that shell—a corrupt and inefficient palace guard —was unable to follow its own interests, let alone the interests of allies.[32] Jefferson realized that he was criticizing a system

31. Malone, *Jefferson and the Rights of Man*, pp. 196–97. Peterson, "Thomas Jefferson and Commercial Policy," pp. 599–600.
32. TJ to Wythe, August 13, 1786, Boyd, *10*, 244.

which taxed a productive middle class while exempting the unproductive but wealthy nobility and clergy; which permitted itself to become dependent upon potential enemies for certain supplies while jealously protecting colonial monopolies; and which looked with mistrust upon any suggestion of free trade that might relieve the country of financial distress and the necessity to trade with the possibly inimical British.

Despite the leadership of the able Vergennes, France's political policy was almost as confused as her economic policy. At one and the same time France wanted the United States to be strong enough to serve as a foil to Britain, and weak enough to remain dependent upon French economic and political support. Although France wanted payment for American debts, she would rather forgo it than accept the money from too strong and independent a central government. Such motives tended to be self-defeating because they blinded statesmen of both nations to the fundamental fact that the United States and France were working toward the same end: the transference of the American economy from the British orbit to that of the French. Their flexible foreign policy made no sense when combined with an antiquated and inflexible economic one. French policy makers failed to recognize that if France loosened her commercial regulations in favor of American trade, as Jefferson advocated, she would gain a far tighter control over American commerce and even American politics.

Confusion of purpose exhibited by the framers of French policy assumed even greater proportions as it spread among members of the discontented merchant class, which had been so long abused by the regime that it did not know how to direct its anger into the proper channels. The merchants—who would have been the first to profit from a free exchange of American tobacco, whale oil, and rice, and the products of France and her colonies—resented the free trade movement out of fear of foreign competition. Inured by habit and prejudice to the ways of mercantilism, they saw in free trade only an opportunity for Britain to inundate France with manufactured goods that

would undersell the products of French manufacturers.[33]
Hence they were not prepared to distinguish between the
doctrinaire spirit of the physiocrats, which looked to free trade
on principle, and the enlightened imperialism of Lafayette,
which sought commercial privileges for the United States as a
powerful weapon against British interests.

An example of the indiscriminate nature of the merchants'
attacks was the flood of protests from chambers of commerce
all over France against trade concessions to Americans in
France, against even the slightest gesture toward admission
of American ships and products in the West Indies.[34] French
representatives in America, like François Barbé-Marbois and
Louis-Guillaume Otto, well understood that if America was to
be won over to France's sphere of influence it was essential
that she be permitted to trade in the part of the French Empire
most essential to her needs.[35] Such observations had little effect
against the logic of mercantilism. Admission of American products into the West Indies would deprive sailors of jobs, would
hurt native business enterprise, and would loosen the ties between colony and motherland; would, in short, destroy the
purpose for which the colonies were originally founded.[36]
These arguments may well have been sound according to the
principles of mercantilism; but the situation of France in the
1780s called for a drastic revision of old shibboleths. The
France of Louis XVI was unable to meet the challenge of the
times.

33. F. L. Nussbaum, *Commercial Policy in the French Revolution: A Study
of the Career of G. J. A. Ducher* (Washington, D.C., 1923), p. 40. The unhappy shortrun consequences of the Anglo-French commercial treaty of
1786, with its physiocratic influence, added fuel to the fire.

34. Memorial of Amiens Chamber of Commerce against introduction of
foreign ships into the West Indies, January 25, 1785, France, Archives des
Affaires Étrangères, *Correspondance politique: États-Unis* (Paris), *29,* 32–38
(photostat copy in the Library of Congress). Hereafter cited as AAE CP E-U.
Complaints of representatives of Le Havre, February 17, 1785, ibid., *29,* 56.

35. Barbé to Vergennes, July 14, 1784, ibid., *28,* 385; Otto to Montmorin,
June 1, 1787, ibid., *32,* 270.

36. Memorial of Amiens Chamber of Commerce, ibid., *29,* 32–38.

Although Jefferson was never fully aware of the extent of France's weakness and duplicity, he was not an undiscriminating adherent of the Revolution politically any more than he was philosophically. On the contrary, he recognized that under any ruler France's policies could conflict with the aspirations of the United States. The alliance with France notwithstanding, Jefferson's suspicions of imperialism were sufficiently aroused by a report of a French scientific expedition to the South Seas in 1785 for him to ask John Paul Jones to find out if the expedition had any designs on the west coast of America.[37] Furthermore, Jefferson was willing to exploit the initial weakness that follows any upheaval, while he waited to exploit the future strength of a reformed France. With apparent pleasure he expected famine and financial bankruptcy to yield America the opening of Santo Domingo, the restoration of whale oil privileges, and even the supplying of starving Paris with salted provisions to be admitted duty free.[38]

But the French were not mistaken in considering Jefferson a friend, for despite these considerations of self-interest the main hopes of the American Minister were centered in the new popular government, composed in large measure of America's friends, which would rebuild on the ruins of a mercantilism a structure of political and commercial collaboration between the two countries firm enough to secure the United States from future attacks by Britain.

Any American in France during the summer of 1789 might be excused for a momentary loss of balance in judging the significance of the Revolution, and Jefferson's aberration was not of long duration. His skepticism about French capacity for self-government never left him. When the National Assembly proudly proclaimed its Declaration of the Rights of Man and its plan for a liberal regime, he noted that our government

---

37. TJ to John Paul Jones, August 3, 1785, Boyd, *8*, 339; TJ to John Jay, August 14, 1785, ibid., *8*, 373–74.
38. TJ to Jay, November 29, 1788, ibid., *14*, 304–05; TJ to Jay, September 19, 1789, ibid., *15*, 456; TJ to Jay, September 30, 1789, ibid., *15*, 502.

"has been professedly their model, in which such changes are made as a difference of circumstances rendered necessary and some others neither necessary nor advantageous, but into which men will ever run, when versed in theory and new in the practice of government, when acquainted with man only as they see him in their books and not in the world."[39] To avoid these dangers, France must rally behind his friends, the moderate royalists and moderate republicans, who alone could defend the successes of the Revolution from the expected attacks of the aristocrats from above and the mobs from below.[40]

Jefferson's fascination with the efflorescence of the French Revolution directly affected the advice he freely offered to the architects of the new government. In 1787 he considered tax reforms and provincial assemblies to be the first step in France's slow evolution toward constitutional government; in 1788 he advanced the progress of her evolution by suggesting a proto-parliament in the form of an Estates-General that possessed the right of taxation; in June, 1789 he perceived the Estates-General as a full-blown legislature; and in August, 1789 he accepted the new government's promulgation of a Declaration of Rights and plans for a constitution that would even limit the king's power over foreign relations. Although his changing views of aspects of French political reform reflected an instability which was undoubtedly the result of emotions unleashed by the Revolution, the ultimate object of his advice remained unchanged: the creation of a constitutional monarchy modeled after Britain's, but purged of British flaws. The revisions in his plan inspired by the progress of the Revolution concerned primarily the time that would be required for France

39. TJ to Madison, August 28, 1789, ibid., *15*, 365.
40. TJ to Jay, September 19, 1789, Boyd, *15*, 458–60. TJ's sympathies were clearly known to both friends and enemies of the Revolution. A group of "patriots," which included the moderate royalist Lafayette and the moderate republican Barnave, used his home as a common meeting ground of two dissenting factions. Another group under the Archbishop of Bordeaux wanted the *"lumières"* of Jefferson's reason and experience for advice on the framing of the Declaration of Rights. See Archbishop of Bordeaux to TJ, July 20, 1789, ibid., *15*, 291; also TJ, *Autobiography*, L&B, *1*, 154–57.

to achieve this goal. Thus, even if Jefferson's resistance to the charms of the French Revolution was at times low, he never changed his original conception of France's political needs, and never confused her revolution with the American Revolution.[41] When he left France in the fall of 1789, the government he left behind was still a monarchy, only mildly limited in powers, supported by a legislature that owed its position to a wealthy electorate representing a small percentage of the nation's population.

Jefferson's constant vigilance for America's interests in all his relations with France accounted for the paradox contained in his personal reactions to the French Revolution. The Revolution had a far greater effect upon his opinions of events in America than it had upon his opinions of contemporaneous developments in France. Fear of alienating the support of French liberals rising to power with the Revolution made him look upon the suppression of Shays' Rebellion and the creation of the Constitution as threats to America's republicanism and hence to America's continued friendship with France. With the exception of occasional lapses in judgment caused by his proximity to the source of the Revolution, the American Minister maintained his objectivity in his understanding of that phenomenon. Conscious of his own historic role as adviser in the remaking of France, he urged his friends to assimilate the benefits of their revolution slowly and to make no attempt to go as far as the United States along the road of political liberty.

The reason behind his plea for moderation was his foreboding that indulgence in excess would destroy the fabric of the new government and render the nation helpless before a restoration of tyranny, in either old or new form. It followed that the destruction of the moderate reforms of 1789 would destroy also the type of alliance that Jefferson had hoped to arrange be-

41. Robert R. Palmer's "The Dubious Democrat: Thomas Jefferson in Bourbon France," *Political Science Quarterly*, 72 (1957), 388–404, is an extended discussion of Jefferson's observations and behavior in France which places more emphasis on Jefferson's doubts than on his enthusiasms.

tween the two countries. Although it was true that he placed no special faith in French promises and that he cynically prepared to exploit French weaknesses, he never wavered in his belief that America's prosperity, if not survival, depended upon the strength of France. With the future of his own country in mind, Jefferson gave wholehearted support to the revolutionists in their struggle against the internal hostility of the privileged classes and the external enmity of the rest of Europe. Powerful as the impact of the French Revolution was upon him as an individual, it affected him primarily as a statesman guarding America's interests in a hostile world.

3.

Jefferson the Statesman: 1789–1794

Odysseus returning home to Ithaca after twenty years of wandering around the Mediterranean could not have been more disappointed with the conditions he found there than Jefferson returning to the United States after an absence of five years in Europe. Since the concept of domestic bliss was magnified in the minds of both men by the hardships of separation, their disillusionment was all the more intense. Odysseus, finding his long-suffering wife besieged by an army of ardent suitors, was forced to mobilize his strength and cunning to do battle after he thought his fighting days had come to an end. Jefferson, finding his beloved homeland threatened by the evil powers of monarchy and aristocracy, girded himself in like manner to wage the good fight once again.

With the cheers of Frenchmen still ringing in his ears and the success of their Revolution stimulating his own enthusiasm for popular government, the new Secretary of State was surprised at the attitude of the people he found about him when he arrived in New York in the spring of 1790. Instead of crowds rejoicing in the possession of liberties for which the French had only begun to reach, he saw the articulate elements of society aping the aristocratic customs of the British enemy. The government, furthermore, seemed to regard itself more the protector of order and property than the guardian of revolutionary ideals.[1]

1. TJ, "Anas," L&B, *1*, 270–71.

His mistrust was aggravated by the cold reception given his program of utilizing France as a counterbalance to English commercial and political power. He conceived as one of his chief duties the cultivation of close ties with France, not to entangle America in European problems but to escape the economic slavery that Britain planned for the United States. The leaders of the new government had no intention of identifying American interests with those of France in any field. The political model of their chieftain, Alexander Hamilton, was the English Constitution, and their goal was the establishment of a relationship with Britain that would guarantee the economic security of both the Federal government and the merchant class which supported it. The lengths to which Hamilton would go in pursuit of Anglophilism extended to the function of secret agent in the service of Great Britain, most notably during the Nootka Sound crisis of 1790 and Jay mission of 1794.[2]

The schism between Jefferson and Hamilton was inevitably personal as well as political. The Secretary of State, a lonely figure in a hostile Cabinet, could not but resent a Secretary of the Treasury who surpassed him in power and prestige, though his junior in years and in political rank. Hamilton's ability to win the President's confidence, the success of his financial schemes, and his genius in administering them stimulated the formation of an opposition party. Jefferson sensed that he could have the support of farmers, who disliked the Federal mercantile aristocracy, and of the masses of people, who were seduced by the magnetic attraction of the French Revolution. These people would be natural allies for Americans who looked to France for support against the plots of the Republic's enemies. Jefferson's championing of the French Revolution, in a manner he had not anticipated when in France, was inspired

2. Julian P. Boyd, *Number 7: Alexander Hamilton's Secret Attempts To Control American Foreign Policy* (Princeton, 1964); Samuel Flagg Bemis, *Jay's Treaty: A Study in Commerce and Diplomacy* (New York, 1923), pp. 343–45.

in part by an understandable jealousy of his adversary's brilliance.

Having served as interpreter of American liberties in France, Jefferson intended to defend those liberties in America. Goaded by personal pride and political circumstances as well as by honest convictions, he joined Madison, as Odysseus had joined Telemachus, to save his Penelope—the fair American republic whose health and beauty he held in so pure an image during his years abroad.

Insight into Hamilton's motive for advocating a customs tariff and the funding of foreign and domestic debts did not come to Jefferson immediately. Remembering the difficulties he had undergone in France because of America's economic and financial weakness, Jefferson at first favored parts of Hamilton's program on the grounds that they would supply the government with sufficient power to command respect.[3] Despite instinctive distrust of the Anglophilism and the aristocratic bias of his Cabinet colleagues, he recognized that the majority of his countrymen shared his fear of Britain and his admiration for the accomplishments of France. The Congress, moreover, was not yet dedicated to Federalist principles. It had already attempted to place restrictions upon English commerce, proposing in one instance to prevent the shipment of American goods in vessels of nations not in treaty with the United States, and in another to prohibit the carrying of American goods in ships of nations which refused to allow their goods to be transported in American vessels. These propositions failed, but in the summer of 1790 the Secretary of State had reason to hope that other forms of retaliation against British commercial measures might have more effect. In any event, he was willing to concede that his opponents, in the Congress at least, might still be "good men and bold men, and sensible men."[4]

3. TJ to George Mason, June 13, 1790, Boyd, *16*, 493; TJ to Monroe, June 20, 1790, ibid., *16*, 537.
4. TJ to Edward Rutledge, July 4, 1790, ibid., *16*, 601.

Jefferson's tone of moderation and understanding gradually turned, during the fall and winter of 1790, into one of bitterness and resentment as he became aware that the Hamiltonian system favored a political economy that was obnoxious to him personally and hostile to his conception of America's best interests. Only after he was convinced that the Federalist minority had nullified the efforts of men of good will in Congress by perverting seemingly wise measures to the exclusive advantage of the commercial-financial class did he join with the unfavored elements of the nation—Southerners, farmers, democrats—in the creation of the Republican opposition party.

Although the French Revolution was only one of the issues over which the Republicans intended to challenge their enemies, it assumed a greater importance than any other issue because it exposed most clearly the vulnerability of the Federalists to attack. The Revolution had captured the imagination of the American people in 1790 and 1791 as it became identified for them with America's own glorious days of a few years back. Jefferson sensed the situation and intended to exploit it. If his response met the demands of political expediency, it also represented his own sincere convictions. America needed France to help preserve her own free institutions, which Jefferson saw threatened by a sect that intended to recreate the English system of government in the New World. To prevent this catastrophe as well as to promote the interests of his party, Jefferson proposed as one solution an "augmentation of the numbers in the lower House, so as to get a more agricultural representation, which may put that interest above that of the stockjobbers." Another preventative would be the firm establishment of the new government of France, for should that be unsuccessful its fate would retard the spread of liberty in other lands and imperil the liberty even of the United States. "I consider," he warned, "the establishment and success of their government as necessary to stay up our own, and to prevent it from falling back to that kind of half-way house, the English constitution." [5]

5. TJ to George Mason, February 4, 1791, L&B, *8*, 124–25.

Once Jefferson had crystallized this position, he took prompt action against his adversaries. His first step was to find a writer who could successfully rebut the Federalist press of Philadelphia, in which he beheld the handiwork of Hamilton and Adams. With the help of Madison he persuaded the poet-editor Philip Freneau, a Princeton classmate of Madison, to set up a paper, the *National Gazette,* and to accept a post as translating clerk in the Department of State.[6]

Within the confines of rival journals party controversy raged on every level; but, as has been suggested, the main issue was not constitutionality of executive powers or the injustices of funding. It was the flaming comet of the French Revolution, dreaded by the Federalists as the omen of anarchy and atheism and praised by the Republicans as both the reflection and the support of the American Revolution. In the wake of its tail, the partisan journalists were able to increase the circulation of their papers as they appealed to the passions of the people.

Jefferson's hope was that the fires of political controversy stirred up by his friends would permit the success of his program without involving him personally in the struggle. Writing articles and engaging in polemical debates were not only distasteful to him but politically unnecessary as long as he could command the services of subordinates to do that work.[7] His hope was not fulfilled. He failed to take into account the responsibilities of leadership which held him accountable for his every word and which made him the major target of all his enemies. Innocently —or at least unwillingly—Jefferson was hurled into the midst of the quarrel by his praise of Thomas Paine's *Rights of Man,* in which the Secretary of State incidentally made a general condemnation of "political heresies" that had appeared in the United States. Paine's fiery pamphlet, written in answer to

6. TJ to Philip Freneau, February 28, 1791, ibid., *8,* 133. Freneau to TJ, March 5, 1791, Jefferson Papers (Library of Congress), *61;* hereafter cited as Jefferson Papers (L.C.). Madison to TJ, May 1, 1791, *Writings of James Madison, 6,* 46. Madison to TJ, July 24, 1791, Madison Papers (Library of Congress). See also Noble Cunningham, *The Jeffersonian Republicans: The Formation of Party Organization, 1789–1801* (Chapel Hill, 1957), pp. 13–20.

7. TJ to Freneau, March 13, 1792, Jefferson Papers (L.C.), 72.

Edmund Burke's strictures on the French Revolution, had been subject to intense attacks in Federalist journals. Sharpest of the critics was one "Publicola," whose style was so similar to that of the well-known "Davila" (John Adams' pseudonym) that Jefferson immediately identified "Publicola" with the Vice-President.[8] It was with John Adams mistakenly in mind that Jefferson provided the editor of the American edition of the pamphlet a prefatory testimonial assailing the critics of Paine's defense of the French Revolution. He was probably sincere in disclaiming foreknowledge of the publication of his note and the public attention it would receive. The sentiments expressed were his, but he seems to have intended them for private circulation and not as a preface to Paine's tract. No matter how angry he was with his old friend Adams' "apostasy to hereditary monarchy," he had no wish to expose himself to the type of abuse an attack *ad hominem* would inspire.[9]

Half-hearted apologies to Adams notwithstanding, Jefferson was unable to extricate himself from the embarrassing situation in which his role as public defender of the French Revolution placed him with his Federalist colleagues. Social isolation in aristocratic Philadelphia and political ineffectiveness in the Hamilton-dominated Cabinet were the price he had to pay for his enlisting France as a political ally. Despite personal discomfort during the remainder of his service as Secretary of State, he did not consider the price excessive.

Obviously some of the bitterness engendered by partisan strife must have seeped into the area of foreign affairs, giving a personal aspect to Jefferson's official relations with France. Even if the ideological and political factors influencing Jefferson as an individual are disregarded, it is evident that his

8. TJ to Washington, May 8, 1791, L&B, *8,* 192. In this letter TJ explained his position in regard to Paine's pamphlet. He did not yet know that "Publicola" was actually John Quincy Adams, the young son of the Vice-President.

9. TJ to Washington, May 8, 1791, ibid., *8,* 193. He made his apologies to Adams two months later for the publicity given his note. TJ to John Adams, July 17, 1791, ibid., *8,* 212–14.

foreign policy was clearly based on close ties with France as a counterbalance to England. As long as England remained America's chief enemy in the eyes of the Secretary of State, the object of his foreign policy would be a relaxation of the economic and political grip of Britain upon the United States. To achieve this purpose, he looked forward to the day when France would absorb American goods hitherto destined for Britain and would provide in return, on terms of equality, manufactured products hitherto obtainable only in Britain.[10] What, then, would account for the objective and often unsympathetic eye which Jefferson cast upon France and the European balance of power at the very time when he was dependent upon the French Revolution for foreign as well as domestic services?

The principal key to Jefferson's attitude toward France during his first two years in office was his conviction that the French Revolution was securely established and progressing at a steady pace.[11] He could therefore afford to be sanguine about the individual problems facing his French friends in adjusting to the new order, and even to be airy about France's national problems, without having to worry about the effects of a possible collapse of the new regime upon the security of his party and country. To Lafayette he suggested that the October disturbances of 1789 were only a sign that a nation should not "expect to be translated from despotism to liberty in a featherbed."[12] To his former patronesses, Mesdames de Houdetot, de Corny, and de Tessé, he was almost callous in his comments upon their sufferings at the hands of the Revolution. He responded to Mme. de Corny's tribulations with a glittering generality and a prayer for her ultimate vindication: "A revolution so pregnant with the general happiness of the nation, will not in the end injure the interests of persons who are so friendly to the general good of mankind as yourself and M. de Corny."[13]

10. TJ to Clavière, August 16, 1792, Jefferson Papers (L.C.), 77.
11. William Short to TJ, December 25, 1789, Boyd, *16*, 43–47; TJ to Thomas Mann Randolph, Jr., March 28, 1790, ibid., *16*, 278.
12. TJ to Lafayette, April 2, 1790, ibid., *16*, 293.
13. TJ to Madame de Corny, April 2, 1790, ibid., *16*, 290.

This sort of language provided little consolation for their losses, and they were inclined to resent his olympian tone. Madame de Houdetot wondered whether his obtuseness was not the result of his American origins; he came from a land where there was little to destroy, where a revolution had only a small job to do.[14]

These letters were written shortly after his return from France, before he had taken any political stand at home, and they probably reflected an absorption with new interests that pushed his French friends into the background. They also reflected his belief in the ability of the Revolution to survive and to make restitution for temporary damage to individuals. In the same manner and for the same reason he exhibited an apparent disregard for the French nation herself—her feelings, and even her aspirations insofar as these infringed upon American interests. Despite his increasing admiration for and dependence upon the symbol of the French Revolution in the United States, he had sufficient confidence in the solidity of the revolutionary structure to subordinate the symbol to his earlier design for utilizing France as a benefactor and tool of the United States.

As if to prove his faith in the ultimate strength of France, he almost welcomed the war cloud that hung over Europe in 1790 as Britain and Spain prepared to contest control of Nootka Sound on the west coast of America.[15] If Spain and Britain actually came to blows over the issue, he felt that France would join the fight as Spain's ally. And he was not concerned. "In that case," he suggested, "I hope the new world will fatten on the follies of the old. If we can but establish the principles of armed neutrality for ourselves, we must become the carriers for all parties as far as we can raise vessels."[16] His apparent

14. Houdetot to TJ, September 3, 1790, ibid., *17*, 486; Gilbert Chinard, ed., *Les amitiés américaines de madame d'Houdetot, d'après sa correspondance inédite avec Benjamin Franklin et Thomas Jefferson* (Paris, 1924), pp. 55–56.

15. William Ray Manning, "Nootka Sound Controversy," American Historical Association, *Annual Report*, 1904 (Washington, D.C., 1905), 279–478.

16. TJ to Rutledge, July 4, 1790, Boyd, *16*, 601.

relish for the distress of Europe was occasioned not by indifference or hostility to France but by his persuasion that the French Revolution had advanced so far that "it cannot be disturbed by a war."[17] France could be exploited, therefore, as an ally of Spain, to win port facilities for the United States at the mouth of the Mississippi. Jefferson reasoned that if France entered the war, Spain would be obligated to accede to her wishes. Ultimate Spanish appeasement in the Nootka Sound controversy ended the threat of war, and hence his optimism was not put to a test.[18]

The fundamental assumption of French national stability also gave the Secretary of State freedom to express himself toward the revolutionary government of France more sharply than he had ever spoken about the *Ancien Régime*. Peculiar though this situation may appear, it is actually more understandable than the objectivity with which he regarded the vicissitudes of France's foreign policy. For Jefferson the revolutionary regime of the National Assembly had none of the excuses of the old government to explain its thwarting of his plans. It was the fruit of a revolution that had looked to the United States and to Jefferson himself for inspiration, and it was composed of men who were personally and philosophically friendly to the United States. It should have been only a question of time, therefore, before an enlightened France would open all her colonies to American trade and would free American commerce from the mischievous restrictions imposed by her earlier government.

When the desired results were not immediately forthcoming, Jefferson suggested to his onetime protégé William Short, American *Chargé d'Affaires* in France, that he apply some pressure to focus the attention of the Assembly upon the needs of the United States. Inasmuch as France was greatly interested in the outcome of the new American loan of three million florins then being negotiated in Amsterdam, Short might sug-

17. TJ to John Harvie, Jr., July 25, 1790, ibid., *17*, 270; TJ to Francis Eppes, July 25, 1790, ibid., *17*, 266.
18. TJ to William Short, August 10, 1790, ibid., *17*, 121–23.

gest that a favorable disposition of American commercial problems with the French West Indies would expedite the payment of the American debt.[19] The Secretary had already supported a measure that did focus the attention of the French government upon the United States: he had encouraged the congressional appointments of Sylvanus Bourne and Fulwar Skipwith to American consulships at Santo Domingo and Martinique respectively.[20] Antoine de Laforest, the French consul in New York, immediately challenged the action on the ground that the appointments contradicted French commercial regulations, a view expanded by the indignation of the French Foreign Office into the general proposition that no nation ever allows foreign trade with colonies.[21] Despite the bluster of the French, Jefferson called upon the consular convention of 1788 for his authority and refused to recall Bourne and Skipwith.[22] Ultimately the French government permitted the consuls to remain in the colonies, provided they carry no official title as such.[23] They could be "commercial agents." It was Jefferson's first diplomatic victory.

France's delay in acceding to what Jefferson considered to be a natural right—free trade everywhere—had deeper roots than the mere bureaucratic inefficiency of any inexperienced regime.[24] The new French Republic proved just as reluctant as the old Monarchy to permit this breach in the colonial monopoly. Within a year of Jefferson's becoming Secretary of State, it imposed extra duties on all except French ships carrying commerce to France herself. Short, in his capacity of *Chargé d'Affaires,* objected to this decree, warning Armand, Comte de

19. TJ to William Short, August 26, 1790, ibid., *17,* 433–34.

20. Fleurieu, Minister of Colonies, to Montmorin, February 11, 1791, AAE CP E-U, *35,* 279–80ᵛᵒ comments on Laforest's report that Skipwith and Bourne had been made consuls in June, 1790. His complaint to TJ resulted in the Secretary's vigorous assertion of American rights.

21. Montmorin to Otto, November 13, 1790, ibid., *25,* 198–99ᵛᵒ.

22. TJ to William Short, April 25, 1791, L&B, *8,* 186–87.

23. TJ to Sylvanus Bourne, May 13 and August 14, 1791, in Worthington C. Ford, ed., *The Correspondence of Thomas Jefferson* (Boston, 1916), 46–48. Montmorin to Thevenard, July 30, 1791, AAE CP E-U, *35,* 379ᵛᵒ.

24. TJ to Randolph, May 30, 1790, Boyd, *16,* 450.

Montmorin, the French foreign minister, that these duties would have a harmful effect upon Franco-American relations.[25] Jefferson's reaction was less diplomatic. The French action appeared to him to be the height of stupidity and ingratitude, "such an act of hostility against our navigation, as was not to have been expected from the friendship of that nation."[26]

This provocation, more than any other, forced Jefferson to realize that the brave new world of the French Revolution was not as new as it had seemed at first. The philosophy of mercantilism, with its jealous protectiveness toward colonies and its commercial monopoly, still dominated French economic councils. He was annoyed at France's fears for the West Indies and her inability to appreciate American needs in those islands. Impress upon our French friends, he advised Short, that the West Indies may take joint action with the United States if the National Assembly does not see the light.[27] The alternative to concessions would be retaliation in kind.[28]

One may wonder how Frenchmen in responsible positions viewed Jefferson's attitude toward their country. It must have been confusing to many. At the same time that he was urging France to promote French-American commerce to deliver America from British financial bondage, he raised suspicions of his good intentions, even of his good faith, by demanding consular representation in the West Indies. When accompanied by vague threats of a joint American military or commercial action with the West Indies independent of France, the demands understandably might equate American consuls with agents of subversion in the minds of Frenchmen. To a skeptical observer like Jean de Ternant, the French minister to the United States in 1792, Jefferson's zeal to serve the interests of France was open to question.[29]

25. Short to Montmorin, April 6, 1791, AAE CP E-U, *35*, 330–31ᵛᵒ.

26. TJ to William Short, July 28, 1791, L&B, *8*, 217.

27. TJ to Washington, July 30, 1791, ibid., *8*, 226. It contained a letter intended for Short.

28. TJ to La Motte, August 30, 1791, ibid., *8*, 239–40.

29. Ternant to Montmorin, October 24, 1791, in Frederick Jackson Turner, "Correspondence of the French Ministers to the United States, 1791–1797,"

The basic difficulty between France and the United States was not distrust of Jefferson's friendship but rather the revolutionary renascence of French mercantilism under the auspices of the National and Legislative Assemblies. Mercantilists were among the most ardent supporters of the French Revolution, seeking through revolutionary change a more efficient government to carry out their plans. Lafayette was actually less effective against their power in the National Assembly than he had been against their friends within the *Ancien Régime* in days when passions were less inflamed. Even the more farsighted mercantilists who had no intention of injuring American commerce wanted, as a matter of principle, to deprive American ships of the right to carry their own tobacco to France and to restrain American commerce from supplying its natural market in the West Indies.[30] Although France desired American friendship and support, she was too apprehensive of American ties with Britain and of commercial competition to make the sacrifices necessary for a harmonious relationship.[31]

In the summer of 1792 Jefferson's complex of attitudes toward France underwent a radical change. His earlier approval of the Revolution, which he had vaguely identified with the limited monarchy of 1789, gave way to a passionate acceptance of French republicanism. His cool objectivity toward points of conflict between French and American interests was supplanted by a willingness to serve French needs in a spirit he had not shown before. The reason for this transformation had little connection with the vagaries of domestic problems. Intensifica-

---

American Historical Association, *Annual Report*, 1903 (Washington, D.C., 1904), 2, 6; Ternant to Dumouriez, June 20, 1792, ibid., 2, 133. The addressee of this correspondence was customarily the Minister of Foreign Affairs.

30. Nussbaum, *Commercial Policy*, pp. 194–97.

31. Montmorin expressed the mercantilist position well when he informed TJ that there were definite limits to the concessions France would grant the United States. Montmorin to Otto, November 13, 1790, AAE CP E-U, 25, 198–99[vo].

tion of party conflict in the United States would not have accounted for the passion with which he now attached himself to the fortunes of the Revolution, since the battle between Hamilton and himself had been joined long before 1792 without curbing his criticism of the French regime or inspiring a reevaluation of the French Revolution.

The cause of the change was external. War between revolutionary France and a European coalition of Prussia and Austria destroyed in one stroke the whole basis of his earlier attitude toward France. No longer could he rely upon the presence of a stable government in France to permit him to exploit French friendship for the advantage of his party and country. The very existence of the Revolution was now at stake, and with it the security of American republicanism. Victory of the Coalition, he was convinced, would provide the "monocrats" of America with the inspiration, and possibly with the material means, to institute a monarchy in the United States on the British model.[32] In order to prevent this catastrophe, the Secretary of State was ready to follow any course the Revolution might take to insure its survival.

His loyalty was soon put to a test. War quickly brought to the surface evidence of the subterranean conflict which had long been waged in France between monarchists and republicans, moderates and radicals, nationalists and internationalists. Jefferson, three thousand miles removed from the scene, had little knowledge of this struggle and less understanding of the nature of the various parties which had either emerged or changed since his departure from France. The Revolution had swallowed most of his French friends and he had to rely on William Short for most of his information. He had difficulty distinguishing the federalist, moderate Girondists who were responsible for the war and were friendly to him from the radical nationalist Jacobins. Referring to the Girondists, he noted: "Notwithstanding the very general abuse of the Jacobins,

32. TJ to Lafayette, June 16, 1792, L&B, *8*, 380–81; TJ to Joel Barlow, June 20, 1792, ibid., *8*, 392–93.

I begin to consider them as representing the true revolution-spirit of the whole nation."[33]

In August 1792, an eruption took place which attracted the attention of the world to the internal affairs of that nation. Moderate and radical republicans joined the mob-dominated Paris Commune in deposing and imprisoning the king, in massacring suspected counter-revolutionists, and in replacing the limited monarchy and its Legislative Assembly with a re-public governed by a National Convention endowed with ex-ecutive as well as legislative powers. This was a revolution as profound as that of 1789.

The diplomatist who left France in 1789 would have been horrified by this development. It was the fulfillment of all the warnings he had given to his friends about the consequences of pushing reforms too fast. Should the mobs of Paris control the movement, he had cautioned, they would not be able to absorb their new liberties and would eventually find them-selves enslaved once again, by the lies of a demagogue if not by the arms of a king. Caught unawares by the event, the Secretary of State might well have considered the government of the Terror to be the tragedy he had predicted. He no longer had a mantle of ignorance to protect him from the truth; the details of the horrors were all available to him. Ternant, the French minister to the United States, as well as Short, Jefferson's chief informant in France, quickly and fully expressed their disgust with the situation in France. Even more expressive was the flight of his old friend Lafayette into exile and imprisonment.[34]

Jefferson, however, welcomed with open arms the Girondist party which had pushed France into war and had borne respon-sibility for establishment of the republic. He hailed its members as fellow republicans, counterparts in 1793 of the patriots of

33. TJ to Madison, June 29, 1792, Ford, 7, 131.
34. TJ to Lafayette, June 16, 1792, L&B, 8, 380. The shock should have been all the greater because two months before Lafayette's flight TJ had written a letter of encouragement, hoping that he would lead the French troops to victory against the enemy.

1789, and forgot all his earlier admonitions. Undoubtedly one reason for the hearty welcome he accorded the Girondists was the personal friendship he enjoyed with their leaders, such men as Brissot and Clavière, who had professed humanitarian aims and had sought to revoke the commercial restrictions of their predecessors.[35] Considering this convenient dovetailing of ideological and economic principles, it is not surprising that Jefferson looked favorably upon the Girondists. But it was not personal friendship which made him ignore the ravages of the Terror; he would probably have extended the same cooperation to any faction which promised to uphold the Revolution and to wage war against the reactionary governments of Europe. "The liberty of the whole earth," he told William Short, "was depending on the issue of the contest" between monarchy and republicanism.[36] So completely did his fear of a French defeat capture his imagination that he was willing to accept any form of government in France which would support the ideals of American freedom.[37]

With the fate of the Revolution hanging in the balance, Jefferson accepted the French Republic as an equal of America and prepared to serve France's foreign policy by acting as her apologist in the United States. What he worked for, primarily, was American recognition of the new republic and an admission from the hostile Washington Administration that the United States should provide France with the war materiel which France had provided the United States during the American Revolution. Opposing Hamilton's attempts to invalidate the old treaty of alliance and to refuse a reception to the new French minister to the United States, Jefferson ridiculed the Federalist contention that the destruction of the French monarchy meant the end of the alliance. Rhetorically, he asked:

35. Nussbaum, *Commercial Policy*, pp. 194–97.
36. TJ to William Short, January 3, 1793, L&B, *9*, 10. This letter represented TJ's attempt to restore Short's wavering faith in the Revolution.
37. TJ to Thomas Mann Randolph, January 7, 1793, ibid., *9*, 13.

"Who is the American who can say with truth that he would not have allied himself to France if she had been a republic?"[38]

Actually, it was unlikely that Hamilton had serious intentions of breaking the alliance in this fashion in 1793; both he and Washington had agreed upon the acceptance of a minister from the French Republic before the issue was even raised in the Cabinet. But by keeping the outcome uncertain, Hamilton could increase his bargaining power in contests with Jefferson of more concern to him, most notably the clause on arming privateers in United States ports,[39] in the Franco-American treaty of commerce. Jefferson himself shared some of these concerns. He considered it a mistake to believe that treaties with France or with Holland authorized those countries to arm vessels in the harbors of their treaty partners.[40]

The nub of the matter was not the fact of alliance, but the responsibilities of the alliance in wartime. While Jefferson might occasionally equate the political structures of the two countries, he never carried his zeal for French victory to the point of encouraging America to enter the war.[41] He recognized France's claims upon the United States, and feared that American abstention might indeed hamper France's war effort. British intervention in the war in February 1793 deepened his anxiety over neutrality. Not only did it make French success more necessary; it also could create the occasion for France to request American support in the event the French West Indies were attacked. At the same time, Jefferson deemed neutrality to be in the national interest as much as did any of his Federalist opponents.[42] American involvement, with its invitation to financial bankruptcy and internal chaos as well as to foreign invasion, would be an even greater threat than evasion of the

---

38. TJ's official opinion on the French treaties, April 28, 1793. Ford, 7, 300.

39. Charles M. Thomas, *American Neutrality in 1793: A Study in Cabinet Government* (New York, 1931), pp. 29–33.

40. TJ to Governor of Virginia, May 23, 1793, L&B, 9, 99.

41. TJ to Ternant, August 27, 1792, ibid., 8, 393–94.

42. J. F. Rippy and Angie Debo, "The Historical Background of the American Policy of Isolation," Smith College *Studies* in History, 9 (April–July, 1924), 157.

alliance's obligations. Some statement on neutrality was needed if only to clarify the extent of America's commitment to France under the treaties of 1778. A loose construction could lead the United States into war against Britain.

Thus Jefferson's initial reservations in April 1793 concerned the effects of a proclamation of neutrality upon friend and enemy rather than the imperative of neutrality itself. By using the term, the United States might offend France; more importantly, a ploy in the American opposition to British maritime pretensions would be needlessly lost. If the British desired American neutrality, let them pay for the privilege with concessions to the principles of neutral rights. They should not be presented with a public gift of neutrality before they had even asked for it.[43] Furthermore, such a proclamation would constitute an invasion of Congressional authority. In light of his fears about Hamilton's ulterior designs the compromise statement wherein Washington omitted the word, "neutrality," on April 23 was apparently satisfactory to the Secretary of State.[44] Or at least it was at the moment of issuance, before the general public and the British alike labeled it as a neutrality proclamation with all that the term implies.

Despite conflicting emotions, Jefferson thought he had found a way to help France without sacrificing the neutrality of his own country. His means was an economic weapon that would force Britain to respect American rights on the high seas, and also guarantee to France the supplies necessary to its prosecution of the war. If Britain, in defiance of America's interpretation of international law, continued to prohibit shipments of provisions to France on American vessels, the United States should retaliate by excluding from its ports all British ships and manufactures.[45]

Jefferson's object was to use France's plight as a new means of achieving old goals—the exclusion of Britain from American

43. Peterson, "Thomas Jefferson and Commercial Policy," *12*, p. 687; Thomas, *American Neutrality*, p. 36.

44. Ibid., pp. 46–47.

45. TJ to Madison, March '?', 1793, L&B, *9*, 33–34.

economic life, the encouragement of commercial ties with France, and the avoidance of war. The Presidential proclamation on April 23, 1793, of America's position vis-à-vis the Anglo-French war seemed well suited to the advancement of this program, since it implied a neutrality that would not anger France and asserted a definition of neutral rights that would permit maximum American economic aid to France.[46]

Those Girondist friends of Jefferson who were concerned with conducting the war and governing the French Republic had neither the time nor the inclination to examine the nature of his attitude toward their country. They had grandiose schemes for the liberation of the world from the grip of monarchy, and assumed as a matter of course that their friend would welcome a role in this noble effort.[47] There was certainly no reason for them to warn their minister to the United States, Edmond Charles Genet, that Jefferson might not approve the instructions given to him upon his departure from France.[48] One of Genet's principal objectives was to arrange a new treaty with the United States similar to the one Jefferson himself had once proposed to Ternant.[49] As for the other objectives, such as arming French privateers in American ports and stirring insurrection in British and Spanish territories, these seemed equally calculated to win the fraternal sympathy and support of Jefferson.

First impressions of the thirty-year-old French minister verified all reports he had heard about America's friendship for

46. TJ to Monroe, July 14, 1793, ibid., *9*, 161–62.

47. Frederick Jackson Turner, "The Origin of Genet's Projected Attack on Louisiana and the Floridas," *American Historical Review, 3* (July, 1898), 660.

48. Condorcet to TJ, December 21, 1792, Jefferson Papers (L.C.), *79*. Letter introducing Genet to TJ, expressing the friendship of both the minister and the Girondists for the United States.

49. TJ over a year before had talked with Ternant about the possibility of a new treaty with France in which the commercial privileges of native citizens should be exchanged between the two countries. "Questions to be considered of as to France," November 26, 1791, Ford, *6*, 337; Frederick A. Schminke, *Genet: The Origins of His Mission to America* (Toulouse, 1939), pp. 48–52.

France. The plaudits of the crowds which greeted him from the time of his landing at Charleston in April, 1793 to his arrival in Philadelphia four weeks later might well have turned the head of an older and wiser man than the romantic revolutionist, Genet. At every stop on his triumphal tour to the Capital, groups of citizens wearing the tricolor and cheering the sister republic in Europe vied for the honor of expressing their appreciation of France's gallant fight for the common cause of liberty. Genet, obviously touched by these outbursts of feeling, was convinced that he had sufficient proof of America's cordial disposition toward France, sufficient certainly to permit him to take seriously the words of a Camden, New Jersey, delegation, which assured him that France "has a just claim on our Gratitude for services rendered to us whilst we struggled to emancipate ourselves from Tyranny."[50]

Had Jefferson restrained the impressionable young Frenchman at this point and informed him frankly of the bounds Americans would place on services they would render France in return, he might have prevented some of the errors which the minister later committed and would not have merited the enmity which Genet later bore toward him. Instead of tempering the minister's exuberance, the Secretary of State seemed not a little awed, himself, by the reception given to Genet. Jefferson's description of the popular reaction to the sight of a British prize being shepherded up the Delaware River by a French frigate suggested that he too enjoyed the unusual spectacle of French colors flying above the British.[51] He was impressed also by the report of a conversation between a Virginia friend and Genet—when the latter was passing through Richmond—about the shipment of flour directly to France from local mills, which would make unnecessary the use of Philadelphia mills.[52] But to Jefferson the most favorable omen

50. Citizens of Camden to Genet, April 25, 1793, Genet Papers (Library of Congress).

51. TJ to James Monroe, May 5, 1793, L&B, *9*, 75.

52. R. Gamble to TJ, May 10, 1793, Jefferson Papers (L.C.), *85*; TJ to Gamble, May 19, 1793, ibid., *86*.

of the Genet mission was the Frenchman's insistence that the
United States remain out of the war so that it might the more
efficaciously supply France and her colonies with needed provisions. "In short he offers everything, and asks nothing."[53]

Encouraged by Genet's popularity, Jefferson naturally turned
his thoughts to making political capital of his support. Genet
found in the Secretary of State a confidant who lost no time in
informing him of Hamilton's enmity to France and of his own
disapproval of the President's recent proclamation. Such was
the interpretation that Genet gave to Jefferson's observations.
It became a major source of the minister's bitterness when the
Secretary refused to repeat publicly what he had told him
privately.[54] Genet even claimed that Jefferson's comments on
the President's lacking power to make a proclamation inspired
his fatal attack on Washington.[55] The Secretary also had a
responsibility for French designs upon Louisiana.[56] Although
he did warn Genet against involving the United States in difficulties with Spain by recruiting an invading force within American territory, he nullified whatever benefit the French minister
might have derived from the warning by adding that he "did
not care what insurrections should be incited in Louisiana" so
long as they were not organized on American soil. As a gesture
of support he even encouraged the French adventure by offering
the French agent and explorer, André Michaux, a letter of
recommendation to Governor Shelby of Kentucky.[57]

Jefferson's conduct was improper. It was a blunder of the
first order, not because it represented his lending his office to
the support of France—which he considered, with reason, to be
in the interest of the balance of power—but because he neglected to inform Genet of the limits of American aid to France

53. TJ to Madison, May 19, 1793, L&B, *9*, 97.

54. Genet to Minister of Foreign Affairs, August 15, 1793, Turner, "Correspondence of the French Ministers," p. 241.

55. Genet to TJ, July 4, 1797, Genet Papers (L.C.).

56. Genet to Minister of Foreign Affairs, May 18, 1793, Turner, "Correspondence of the French Ministers," p. 215.

57. TJ, "Anas," July 5, 1793, L&B, *1*, 362–63.

or of the breaking point of national pride. Jefferson in his early interviews with Genet had given that minister the impression that the people, if not the government, would approve his every action. Both Jefferson and his party had eventually to pay in loss of public favor for having misled the French minister. As for Genet, he was justified in accusing Jefferson of betraying him by leading the movement for his recall; but, characteristically, the young diplomat damned him for the wrong reason: that Jefferson had denounced him out of jealousy of his popularity with the American people.[58]

Jefferson repudiated Genet only after the latter, by repeated provocations, had threatened to destroy both America's neutrality and the popularity which the French Revolution had enjoyed with the American people.[59] His policy of aid to revolutionary France had always been contingent upon the preservation of America's neutrality. Even before the arrival of Genet in Philadelphia, Jefferson had been disturbed by the threats to neutrality contained in his disposing of prizes that French warships brought to American ports and in his practice of equipping French privateers there: "Shall we permit her to sell them? The treaty does not say we shall, and it says we shall not permit the like to England. Shall we permit France to fit out privateers here? The treaty does not stipulate that we shall tho' it says we shall not permit the English to do it."[60] Thus at the very time he was friendliest with Genet, Jefferson was seeking means of denying to France an important source of revenue for the pursuance of the war, and of nullifying a vital weapon against British sea power.

Jefferson's purpose in thwarting this segment of Genet's program was simply to forestall conflict, and possibly a war, with Britain that would be no more beneficial to France than to

58. Genet to TJ, July 4, 1797, Genet Papers (L.C.). The theme of Genet's betrayal at the hands of TJ was taken up and mistreated in Meade Minnegerode, *Jefferson, Friend of France, 1793* (New York, 1928).

59. TJ to Monroe, July 14, 1793, L&B, *9*, 164. TJ to Madison, September 1, 1793, ibid., *9*, 212–13.

60. TJ to Madison, April 28, 1793, Ford, *7*, 301–02.

the United States. He sought a solution which would both satisfy Britain and mollify France. He failed.[61] Genet could not believe that the Secretary of State was serious in ordering him to remove illegally equipped privateers from American waters and in prohibiting him in the future from fitting out privateers in American ports. When the young Minister consequently ignored his official requests, Jefferson was forced to resort to the same argument that he had condemned Hamilton for using a few months before. The Secretary appealed to the authority of international law to prove to the French that the entry of their armed vessels into a port in accordance with a treaty regulation was a very different matter from their arming vesels in American ports. His contemptuous dismissal of the "ill-understood scrap of Vattel," on which Hamilton had based his case for refusing recognition to France in April 1793, was replaced in June of that year by a new reverence for the opinions of "enlightened and disinterested Judges," one of whom was the same Vattel![62]

If Jefferson sensed danger to America's neutrality in Genet's behavior, he sensed danger also to his own position as party leader and to France's standing with the American people. He feared that Genet's truculence toward the President would alienate the affection the people had for France and would give added political strength to the Federalist enemies of France and the Republican party.[63] His leadership in procuring Genet's recall was the outcome of this concern.[64] By personally facilitating the exposure of Genet's indiscretions, he attempted to disassociate himself from the minister's actions and to dis-

61. TJ to Madison, June 2, 1793, L&B, 9, 105.

62. TJ to Madison, April 28, 1793, Ford, 7, 301; TJ to Genet, June 17, 1793, L&B, 9, 134–37.

63. TJ to Madison, September 1, 1793, L&B, 9, 212–13.

64. TJ to Gouverneur Morris, August 16, 1793, ibid., 9, 180–209. This letter to the American Minister to France contained a record of the charges against Genet which Morris was to present to the French government. It should be noted that the Jacobin government of France which had deposed Genet's Girondist friends did not sympathize with either the policies or the plight of that minister.

associate France from the stigma of Genet's newly effected unpopularity in America.[65]

From the standpoint of America's best interests, Jefferson's repudiation of Genet was well advised; he had rid the country of a dangerous personality. But the fall of Genet coincided with the termination of his own career as Secretary of State, and much of the obloquy attached to Genet's name rubbed off onto himself. The Federalists had succeeded in using the Genet issue to maintain their dominance in the government and, in addition, seemed to have won Washington to their side as a partisan rather than as a moderator. Jefferson—who had long sought to extricate himself from his painful Cabinet position—was allowed to depart on the last day of December 1793.

Jefferson's objectives as Secretary of State had changed little since 1790; he sought to the very day of his retirement to free the United States from the economic and political grip of Great Britain, and to employ the services of France in effecting this end. What had changed radically between 1790 and 1793 was his conception of the French Revolution, as his understanding of that phenomenon was gradually warped by his distance from the scene, by the needs of his political party, and by the European coalition against France. Inevitably his philosophical prejudices and his partisan considerations influenced his conduct in the arena of foreign affairs, and the failure of the Genet mission bore marks of the intrusion of those influences. His foreign policy nevertheless emerged consistently successful in extracting advantage for America from Europe's difficulties, in upholding the balance of power in Europe by support of France, and in preserving the neutrality of the United States.

65. TJ to Madison, August 11, 1793, Jefferson Papers (L.C.), *91;* Genet to Edmund Randolph, December 16, 1793, Genet Papers (L.C.). Genet accused TJ of reporting to the President that he intended to appeal over the head of the government to the people for support of his policies. Minnegerode (*Jefferson, Friend of France,* pp. 320–35) admitted that Genet did make these threats but declared that TJ had purposely misconstrued them so that they would appear more incendiary than he had intended.

4.

Jefferson the Politician: 1794–1799

The British philosopher–historian, Arnold Toynbee, has advanced the thesis that there is a mystic path to greatness followed by creative personalities which involves the withdrawal of the individual from active relations with society so that he may "realize powers within himself which might have remained dormant if he had not been released for the time being from his social toils and trammels."[1] Men like St. Paul, Mohammed, and Machiavelli have shared, according to Toynbee, the experience of a hiatus in their lives during which time they had deserted the world of affairs to reflect upon their relations with their fellows. Thus the isolation of Paul in the Arabian desert, the departure of Mohammed from Mecca, and the rustication of Machiavelli on a Tuscan farm marked the metamorphosis of Paul from a Pharisee to a Christian organizer, of Mohammed from an unpopular mystic to a powerful leader of a new religion, of Machiavelli from a practical politician to a political philosopher.[2]

Thomas Jefferson, always distrustful of metaphysics and metaphysical speculations, never made an official rationalization of his retirement in 1793, but the tenor of his commentary on his experiences during that period suggests that he had withdrawn from office because of his preference for the reflective

1. Arnold Toynbee, *A Study of History* (Somervell abridgement, New York, 1947), p. 217.
2. Ibid., pp. 225–30.

life and that he had returned to politics at the insistence of his fellow countrymen. Did his years of seclusion at Monticello prepare him for more effective service to his people by giving them time to understand the rightness of his ideas?

There is considerable merit in this interpretation of Jefferson's motives in retiring from the State Department. He was obviously eager to assume the more respected role of philosopher of democracy, and was honestly tired of fighting his powerful opponents from his exposed position in the Cabinet. All his hopes of serving American interests by frustrating the plans of the British bloc seemed quixotic in the face of Hamilton's successful manipulation of the Washington Administration.[3] The heaviest blow of all, perhaps, was his loss of faith in President Washington's impartiality.[4] But his resignation represented no cowardly retreat from political combat.[5] Jefferson had fought for his program long enough and hard enough to deserve the right of awaiting his vindication in the tranquil atmosphere of his Virginia home.

This explanation of his actions does not take into account certain compromising factors. The ideas which he expressed on the eve of his departure from Philadelphia indicate no renunciation of political ambitions. He was counting on a wave of national resentment against new British outrages—such as the British Order-in-Council of June 8, 1793, instructing naval commanders to bring in all neutral ships carrying flour, corn, or meal which were bound for French ports—to counteract the effect of Genet's blunders and to inspire a renascence of his party and his program. Less than a month before his resignation he had urged Washington to publicize the British actions.[6]

3. TJ to Madison, May 13, 1793, Jefferson Papers (L.C.), *85*. W. Woolery ("The Relations of Thomas Jefferson to American Foreign Policy, 1783–1793," *Johns Hopkins University Studies in History and Political Science, 45* [Baltimore, 1927], 118–19) cited Hamilton's interference as a reason for TJ's resignation.

4. TJ to Madison, August 11, 1793, Jefferson Papers (L.C.), *92*.

5. Philip M. Marsh, "Jefferson's Retirement as Secretary of State," *Pennsylvania Magazine of History, 69* (July, 1945), 222–23.

6. TJ to Washington, December 2, 1793, L&B, *9*, 262–64.

Ostensibly he wished the President to bring the issues with Britain before the public so that he might demonstrate his independence of the pro-British party; privately he thought that the exposure of British crimes against America in the Northwest territory, on the high seas, and in the Mediterranean, would inspire the Congress to pass retaliatory commercial measures against Britain.[7]

Since this favorable turn of events occurred at the time he was preparing to lay down the burden of office, it seems unlikely that Jefferson left Philadelphia in despair of his party's future.[8] His own fortunes, for that matter, could prosper in retirement. His friends in Congress did not need his presence to carry out a policy that would both enhance his prestige and damage the popularity of his Anglophile enemies. Anticipating troubles for the Federalists, he may have retired when he did because it was the right psychological moment for him to disassociate himself from the unpopular policies of the Administration.[9]

While there is no evidence to substantiate assertions that his resignation was part of a master plan of the Republicans to mobilize public opinion against the Federalists and the British,[10] there are sufficient data to show that Jefferson was neither unaware of the political significance of the rising tide of Anglophobia nor unwilling to profit from it. His withdrawal to Monticello was only a physical withdrawal; he took politics with him to his mountain retreat.

7. TJ to Martha Randolph, December 22, 1793, Ford, *8*, 125.

8. Dumas Malone, *Jefferson and the Ordeal of Liberty*, Vol. 3 of *Jefferson and His Time* (Boston, 1962), pp. 161–62.

9. Albert J. Beveridge, *The Life of John Marshall* (4 vols. Boston, 1916), 2, 96.

10. Ternant, Genet's predecessor and no friend of TJ, thought that talk of resignation in 1792 was only a feint worked out by Republicans to gain political advantage. Ternant to Minister of Foreign Affairs, January 12, 1793, Turner, "Correspondence of the French Ministers," p. 168. Fauchet, Genet's successor, suggested a year after TJ's departure that his resignation was good politics since he would no longer be identified with Federalist errors. Fauchet to Commissioner of Foreign Affairs, October 31, 1794, ibid., p. 452.

There was in the correspondence of the former Secretary of State an element of dissimulation that can be attributed to self-deception. Jefferson may have convinced himself that he had interest only in agrarian activities and had nothing but contempt for the sordid politics of the city. He repeated this theme often enough. Four months after his retirement he was still protesting as vigorously as on the first day that he was interested exclusively in "the tranquil growth of my lucerne and potatoes."[11]

If he believed these statements, he was obviously ignoring contradictory sentiments expressed in his same letters, as well as in many letters from his Philadelphia correspondents. Although he was literally truthful when he boasted that he had received no city newspapers since his return to Monticello,[12] he had no need of any. Madison, William Branch Giles, and Monroe were keeping him fully informed on every political development in Philadelphia, particularly the outcome of the non-importation bill aimed at Britain.[13] While he was professing exclusive preoccupation with farming, he did not neglect to encourage his friends in Congress with reports of the passionate dislike of his Virginia neighbors for Britain.[14] Nor did he confine his observations to the local Virginia scene; he expressed his concern for America's relations with the West Indies and with Europe in far more vehement terms than he had as Secretary of State.[15]

Jefferson's role as a civilian Cincinnatus might have been maintained if Madison's resolutions of January 3, 1794, for retaliatory duties on British imports had not met unexpected

11. TJ to Tench Coxe, May 1, 1794, L&B, *9*, 285.
12. Ibid., *9*, 285.
13. Giles became TJ's chief Philadelphia correspondent, excepting Madison, after Monroe was appointed Minister to France in May 1794. For TJ's interest in Madison's Non-importation Bill, see Bemis, *Jay's Treaty*, pp. 186–88.
14. TJ to Archibald Stuart, January 26, 1794, Ford, *8*, 137; TJ to James Monroe, April 24, 1794, ibid., *8*, 143–44.
15. TJ to Madison, April 3, 1794, L&B, *9*, 282.

difficulties. The Federalists had closed ranks when they saw their dominance threatened. Monroe indignantly reported the tricks they were using to evade Madison's proposals, such as the scrapping of the Republican program in favor of their own project of raising 15,000 troops to defend the country against potential invasion. They did not really fear invasion, claimed Monroe; what they wanted was the establishment of a military government as a step toward monarchy. Their new posture toward Great Britain was merely a trick to delude Republicans.[16] Actually their most audacious maneuver was the one that succeeded. The Federalists imposed upon a reluctant Congress the Jay mission to England.[17] Fearing war with Britain as the logical outcome of retaliatory action against British spoliations, the Federalists managed to send the Chief Justice to London in a last effort to reach an agreement on the rights of neutrals. Republicans had reason to be chagrined by this arrangement. Their principal weapon against the Federalists was Anglophobia. An honorable settlement with Britain would redound to the advantage of Britain's friends in America and, incidentally, would deprive their leader of the luxury of appearing indifferent to politics.

The Federalists were justified in fearing the possibility of war in 1794, as the combination of British provocation and Republican agitation roused public feeling to a fever pitch. Instead of goading his friends from his rural retreat,[18] Jefferson would have done better to heed the advice of his friendly enemy, John Adams, on the significance of Jay's mission. If Jay were successful, Adams pointed out, the United States would be kept out of a war that, if fought, would add hundreds of millions to the national debt and leave the country exposed to monarchy and aristocracy. "Those who dread Monarchy and Aristocracy and at the same time Advocate War are the most

16. Monroe to TJ, March 16, 1794, in S. M. Hamilton, ed., *The Writings of James Monroe* (7 vols. New York, 1898–1903), *1*, 285–86.

17. Bemis, *Jay's Treaty* (pp. 193–97), gives an account of the "executive manoeuvre" that produced the mission.

18. TJ to Tench Coxe, May 1, 1794, L&B, *9*, 285–86.

inconsistent of all men."[19] Although Jefferson gave no sign of recognizing this rebuke from John Adams, the unexpected Federalist mission which he deplored so vehemently may have been the instrument that saved him from assuming responsibility for a disastrous Anglo-American war. His own claim that the surest road to peace lay in the path of retaliation ignored the danger, of which Adams warned, of further inflaming the passions of an already aroused people.[20]

The treaty which resulted from Jay's mission provoked a storm of criticism that swept the country in the summer of 1795, threatening to destroy Federalism by its fury. The treaty relinquished, for the duration of the European War, free ships, free goods, and the right of neutrals to trade in non-contraband goods. Such humiliating concessions to British sea power shocked both parties momentarily. Even Hamilton condemned the treaty as an "execrable thing."[21]

Despite these exploitable circumstances, the Republicans failed to gain political advantage from their successful policy of stirring up the people against Britain and her American friends, even after the Federalist majority in the Senate accepted the treaty, albeit by a bare margin. Preferring even a bad treaty to a break with Britain, the Federalists blunted popular wrath over their action by pointing to a French insult to American sovereignty that exceeded anything Britain had done. A British warship had seized some compromising dispatches of Fauchet, the French minister to the United States, in the course of a routine examination of ships bound for France. These dispatches, containing reports of conversations between Fauchet and Secretary of State Edmund Randolph concerning their mutual hopes for the defeat of Jay's Treaty, were promptly turned over to the Federalists for immediate exploitation.

19. John Adams to TJ, May 11, 1794, in Lester J. Cappon, ed., *The Adams–Jefferson Letters: The Complete Correspondence between Thomas Jefferson and Abigail and John Adams* (2 vols. Chapel Hill, 1959), *1,* 255.

20. TJ to Washington, May 14, 1794, L&B, *9,* 287–88. See Albert H. Bowman, "Jefferson, Hamilton, and American Foreign Policy," *Political Science Quarterly, 71* (March, 1956), 39–40, for support of TJ's view.

21. TJ, "Anas," August 24, 1797, L&B, *1,* 416.

Washington thereupon signed the treaty, which was as offensive to him as to any Republican, in order to allay charges of French interference in his Administration.[22]

It is ironic that the question of French influence in American politics should have come up in this fashion to spoil Republican plans, especially since Jefferson and his allies had been citing Jay's Treaty as a horrible example of British control of Federalist foreign policy. It is apparent, moreover, that Randolph's conversations with Fauchet were not part of the Jeffersonian program. Although the Secretary of State was nominally a Republican, Jefferson did not trust him; he had always resented his ties with Washington and had been annoyed by his susceptibility to Federalist intimidation when they were colleagues in the Cabinet.[23] Randolph's indiscretions seemed, rather, to have been inspired by his resentment of the power Hamilton exercised in the Department of State—not unlike Jefferson's feeling two years earlier.[24]

The Republican failure to overthrow Federalism led to no re-examination of the usefulness of France as a champion of republican government. Instead of questioning the political value, not to mention the purposes, of his foreign ally, Jefferson lent his prestige to France's efforts to undo Jay's Treaty, in the hope of influencing the presidential election of 1796.

The personal instrument of the French plan was James Monroe, United States minister to France. Monroe was determined to make amends for the monarchical sympathies of his predecessor, Gouverneur Morris. Enthusiastic about the Revolution, he succeeded in convincing the French government of his people's friendship for France but was unable to banish

22. D. Anderson, "Edmund Randolph," in S. F. Bemis, ed., *American Secretaries of State and Their Diplomacy* (10 vols. New York, 1928), 2, 102. A more recent discussion of the Randolph case is Irving Brant, "Edmund Randolph, Not Guilty!" *William and Mary Quarterly*, Third Series, 7 (1950), 179–98. See also Alexander De Conde, *Entangling Alliance: Politics and Diplomacy Under George Washington* (Durham, N.C., 1958), pp. 123–25.

23. TJ to Giles, December 31, 1795, L&B, 9, 314–17.

24. Anderson, "Edmund Randolph," p. 111.

their suspicions about Jay's visit to England. In order to quiet French fears, he asked Jay to tell him the contents of his treaty as soon as possible, but Jay, fearing with good reason the consequences of an immediate revelation, was willing to give him the information only on condition that it would be kept confidential.[25] Monroe refused to accept that stipulation, since he had already assured the French that he would give them the details of the treaty the moment he received them.[26] So long as he did not know what was taking place in London, he could continue to assure them that the treaty negotiations concerned only the settlement of debts and British evacuation of the Northwest posts.[27]

Repudiated by Washington for his undiplomatic assurances to the French concerning Jay's Treaty, Monroe had to face the wrath of France over America's abandonment of resistance to British violations of neutral rights, the cornerstone of Franco-American wartime trade. Far from admitting his mistake in not preparing the French for a situation he had anticipated, the impressionable American minister poured out to Jefferson his bitterness against the ungrateful Administration which had destroyed all the good works he had accomplished in France.[28] In defending his own behavior he compounded his error by convincing the French that the American people were not to blame for what France considered a betrayal of the Treaty of 1778.[29] He retained his popularity in France only at the cost of

25. Monroe to Randolph, February 1, 1795, *The Writings of James Monroe*, 2, 186; Monroe to Randolph, March 17, 1795, ibid., 2, 229–30.

26. James Monroe, *A View of the Conduct of the Executive in the Foreign Affairs of the United States, as Connected with the Mission to the French Republic during the Years, 1794, 5, and 6* (Philadelphia, 1798), p. 19.

27. Ibid., p. 3. See S. F. Bemis, "Washington's Farewell Address: A Policy of Independence," *American Historical Review*, 39 (1934), 254–56.

28. Monroe to TJ, June 23, 1795, *The Writings of James Monroe*, 2, 301–03. B. W. Bond ("The Monroe Mission to France," *Johns Hopkins University Studies in History and Political Science*, 15 [Baltimore, 1907], 47) claims that Monroe's deep sympathy for French aspirations was the source of his indiscretions.

29. Monroe to Madison, January 12, 1796, *The Writings of James Monroe*, 2, 432–33.

instigating the French to take retaliatory steps against the Federalist government. Following Monroe's reasoning, the French leaders assumed that a show of displeasure with Washington's Administration would help Republicans in the United States to oust the Federalists at the presidential polls. By breaking off diplomatic relations with the United States and by threatening war, they felt that they would crystallize popular opposition to Jay's Treaty and guarantee the election of the one man who would be acceptable to them in the office of President. That man was Thomas Jefferson.[30]

The French acted immediately on their project of electing the Virginia farmer to the American Presidency. Their first step was to replace the French minister in the United States, P. A. Adet, with an envoy who would express France's dissatisfaction with Jay's Treaty in strong terms. N. Vincent, Director of Fortification at Santo Domingo, was ordered to proceed at once to the United States.[31] Monroe, in his unofficial capacity of adviser to the French government, opposed the appointment on the grounds of its being bad politics. Feeling against Britain in America was already high enough to insure victory. The representations of a special envoy, he feared, might insult American pride.[32]

The Vincent mission miscarried, but through no help of Monroe; at the time of his appointment Vincent was under suspicion of having tampered with the list of prescribed *émigrés* —a serious offense in a revolutionary government at war.[33] The bureaucrats of the Directory then scrapped the idea of a special mission in favor of an even more pointed means of expressing

30. Report to Executive Directory by Minister of Foreign Affairs, January 17, 1796, AAE CP E-U, *45*, 41–53. De Conde, in *Entangling Alliance*, p. 375, believes that Monroe's action "did avert a crisis his government was unprepared to meet."

31. Secretary General of Executive Directory to Vincent, February 17, 1796, AAE CP E-U, *45*, 150.

32. Monroe to Minister of Foreign Affairs, February 17, 1796, ibid., *45*, 146–47.

33. Vincent to Members of Directory, March 18, 1796, ibid., *45*, 251–52.

France's disapproval of Federalist behavior.[34] They ordered Adet, the minister already in America, to announce dramatically on the eve of the election the suspension of his ministerial functions.[35]

Neither Jefferson in Virginia nor Monroe in Paris appreciated the changes that had taken place in the government of France between 1793 and 1796. The Girondists had given way to a chaotic dictatorship run by short-lived demagogues who in 1795 surrendered the reins of government to a five-man Directory which maintained only the framework of the revolutionary ideals. Like their Girondist predecessors these men had ambitions world-wide in scope but, unlike the Girondist idealists, they envisioned the resurrection of French imperialism rather than the enlargement of individual and national liberties. The objective of the Directory in 1796—an objective unseen by American Republicans—was more than the utilization of the United States as a source of supply, as had been the Girondist plan; it was to bring the United States into the war as an active ally.[36]

Although Monroe attempted to control the sequence of events he had helped to initiate in France, Jefferson, the key figure in France's plans, showed no disapproval of any of the French activities in his behalf. The enterprising Adet had even anticipated his orders by advising the Directory in June, 1796 to make their displeasure with the United States government known to the American people, in order to encourage "the men who are devoted to us."[37] While Jefferson did not know the contents of the communications of the French Foreign Office, and did not even suspect the fundamental reasons for France's

34. Observations of Secretary General of Directory on Monroe's letter, protesting Vincent mission of February 17, 1796, ibid., *45*, 148–49.

35. Minister of Foreign Affairs to Adet, August 24, 1796, ibid., *46*, 144–45. See Bemis, "Washington's Farewell Address," pp. 264–65.

36. Report to Executive Directory by Minister of Foreign Affairs, January 17, 1796, AAE CP E-U, *45*, 41–53.

37. Adet to Minister of Foreign Affairs, June 9, 1796, Turner, "Correspondence of the French Ministers," p. 921.

support of his candidacy, he could not have ignored Adet's personal and active campaigning.[38] The extent of Jefferson's responsibility for French interference in the election cannot be found, however, in any contacts he had with French officials, for he had none. It can be found only in the extent of his knowledge of the political situation of 1796 and of France's relation to it. That knowledge was considerable even though it was not put to good use. What information Monroe did not provide directly he instructed other friends to send on to him. At Monticello Jefferson was more thoroughly informed of Monroe's activities in France than was the State Department. By approving the behavior of the disgraced minister he took upon himself some of the responsibility for the new turn in Franco-American relations.

Jefferson's replies to Monroe's letters reflected his sympathy for his disciple's unhappy position in France and for his mistreatment at the hands of the Federalists. He gave Monroe more than mere sympathy. He encouraged him in his plans for undoing the damage caused by Jay's Treaty by emphasizing the disappointment of the American people with the Administration and his own anger at the effrontery of the Federalists, particularly Hamilton hiding being the pseudonym Camillus, in defending their deal with Great Britain.[39] Apparently Jefferson was too incensed over Jay's Treaty to appreciate the imprudence of Monroe's behavior in France. Instead, he provided the Minister with the impression that the will of one man, the President, had thwarted the will of the people.[40] Madison, wiser than Jefferson at this time and always suspicious of Monroe's judgment, warned of the folly of Monroe's actions, but was unable to dissuade Jefferson from giving advice and

38. Adet to Minister of Foreign Affairs, September 24, 1796, ibid., p. 948; Adet to Minister of Foreign Affairs, November 22, 1796, ibid., p. 972. See also Hamilton to Rufus King, December 16, 1796, in Henry Cabot Lodge, ed., *The Works of Alexander Hamilton* (12 vols. New York, 1904), *10*, 215.

39. TJ to Monroe, September 6, 1795, Ford, *8*, 186–87; TJ to Monroe, March 2, 1796, ibid., *8*, 221.

40. TJ to Monroe, June 12, 1796, L&B, *9*, 337; TJ to Monroe, July 10, 1796, ibid., *9*, 348.

encouragement when the disgraced diplomat returned to the United States to attack Washington and the Federalists. Jefferson did advise Monroe, however, to use caution in attacking such a popular figure as Washington.[41]

What Monroe had wrought with Jefferson's full cooperation was a joint campaign of the French and the Republicans to put their candidate in office. Jefferson claimed that he was not a candidate. In early summer of 1796 all talk of crass politics disappeared from his correspondence, as if he had never before discussed Jay's Treaty with his friends. He was once again the busy farmer so indifferent to everything except agriculture that when the nomination was proffered he exclaimed that his name had been brought forward "without concert or expectation" on his part.[42]

Whatever may have been his feeling about the burdens of office-holding, he had knowingly accepted the aid of France in seeking the presidency. His awareness of political opportunities did not help him to understand, however, that French support of the Republicans served to elect John Adams to the Presidency. Adet was too insistent upon a Jeffersonian victory as the only way for America to appease France's wrath, and Benjamin Franklin Bache's Republican newspaper, the *Aurora,* went too far in its attacks upon Washington's character. Instead of frightening the people into submission, French actions merely stiffened American resistance to the demands of the Directory and distracted the nation's attention from British insults and Federalist Anglophilism. The key to Adams' victory seems to have been the firm hand of Washington pointing out the path which America wished to follow. In his Farewell Address he defended the foreign policy of his Administration and repeated

41. Madison to TJ, October 20, 1797, Madison Papers (L.C.), 20. TJ to Monroe, October 25, 1797, Ford, *8,* 344–45.

42. TJ to Jonathan Williams, July 3, 1796, L&B, *9,* 346; TJ to Edward Rutledge, December 27, 1796, ibid., *9,* 353. Adrienne Koch (*Jefferson and Madison: The Great Collaboration* [New York, 1950], p. 164) believes that TJ's desire that Madison be the Republican candidate was completely sincere. Malone (*Jefferson and the Ordeal of Liberty,* p. 273) asserts that he was "actually a nonparticipant" in the election activities.

the ideas underlying his Neutrality Proclamation of 1793 by urging American isolation from the quarrels of Europe and avoidance of entangling alliances. The object lesson for Americans implied in that speech was the unfortunate experience with the French alliance and its consequences—France's interference in America's domestic affairs.[43]

If Washington's analysis of America's true interests was correct, Jefferson appears to have neglected the balance of power in 1796. Even if he had made no personal contact with French officials, his toleration of their efforts in his behalf would have placed him under obligation to a power which had converted a war of national defense into a war of aggression. As master of Europe, France could turn on her weak ally with no third force to stop aggression on the American side of the Atlantic. But whether France won her struggle or not, Jefferson's sense of duty and his idea of the national interest might have plunged the United States into a war with Britain which would have ruined America's prosperity as well as jeopardizing her very sovereignty. In either case his personal entanglement with France had endangered the security of his country.

The attitude of France toward the United States altered considerably from 1792 to 1798, almost as radically as did her government. The Convention of 1792 and 1793 looked upon the United States as a source of supply for the West Indies and for France's war machine; the Directory in 1795 and 1796 saw a possible ally actively participating in a war in which the outcome was uncertain; the Directory in 1797 and 1798, commanding the finest armies in Europe, sought only to avoid war with America, at least for the time being, so that its own ambitions for a new empire would remain undisturbed.

Beneath these policy changes there was one factor in Franco-American relations that remained constant: France's confidence

43. Bemis, "Washington's Farewell Address," p. 262. Alexander De Conde in "Washington's Farewell Address, the French Alliance, and the Election of 1796," *Mississippi Valley Historical Review, 63* (1957), 648–50, notes the partisan Federalist element in the Address.

that a strong French party existed in America which held sufficient power and influence to give her freedom of action in her
dealings with the United States. Jefferson was the leader of that
party, the rock on which successive French governments built
their projects for revoking Jay's Treaty, for supplying their
colonies, and even for providing bribes on suitable occasions.

There were dissenters among French observers, who doubted
Jefferson's altruism in regard to his friendship for France. The
Duc de la Rochefoucald, a liberal aristocrat in American exile,
considered him to be less pro-French than Hamilton was pro-
British. He was neither a revolutionist nor a monarchist but a
true republican and a loyal American, claimed this friend of
Jefferson.[44] Adet, the French minister who campaigned for
Jefferson's election in 1796, noted the same qualities, although
as a government official he was not happy in the realization
that Jefferson loved France only because he feared and detested
Britain. The fact that the Virginian had a special interest
motivating his friendship was reason enough for Adet to assert
that France could rely upon no American for unqualified support.[45]

Essentially both men were correct in noting that Jefferson
was, above all else, an American, seeking America's advantage
out of his relations with France. They erred in not recognizing
that he was unable to distinguish national interests from his
party's interests, or party interests from French interests, at this
moment. Adet's comment, made at the conclusion of an unsuccessful election campaign, was wide of the mark, for the new
Vice-President's stake in the defeat of England made him poten-
tially more useful to France's imperial ambitions.

Following the failure of the policy of intimidation, the Directory adopted a new program which reflected a change both in
purpose and in method in France's treatment of the United
States. With respect to method, the reports of junior diplo-

44. F. A. F. de la Rochefoucald-Liancourt, *Travels Through the United States, 1795, 96, 97* (2 vols. London, 1799), 2, 77–79.
45. Adet to Minister of Foreign Affairs, December 31, 1796, Turner, "Correspondence of the French Ministers," pp. 982–83.

matists and special agents in the United States convinced the government that Genet's and Adet's interference in American politics served only the interests of Britain and the Federalists. With respect to purpose, the Directory realized in 1797 that it had no need of the military services of the small overseas republic. As the most powerful nation in Europe, France could concern herself with new conquests and not with mere survival, and required for this project, which included the reclamation of Louisiana, only the neutrality of the United States.[46]

The idea of winning back the empire France had lost to Spain and Britain in 1763 was not new. Since that year every French government had given some thought to its restoration. The Girondists through Genet and their agents in America had made specific plans for its conquest as far back as 1792, but their plans had an idealistic basis encompassing the emancipation of the territory to the advantage of its citizens and of the United States as well as of France. The Directors, on the other hand, frankly wanted Louisiana as part of a new empire, and were under no illusions about receiving America's blessings for their aspirations.[47] They recognized the need of a friendly and unsuspecting America that would not be tempted to engage in any adventures with Britain which might involve seizure of the territory before French diplomacy or French armies could win it for France. To mask their plans they intended to jettison the old policy of intimidation and spoliation, but they did not intend to dispense with the services of Jefferson's party.

If Jefferson in retirement was an inspiration to the French, Jefferson as Vice-President of the United States should logically have been of still more use. He certainly did all in his power to assure them that their plans would have his complete support.

46. Letombe to Minister of Foreign Affairs, June 7, 1797, Turner, "Correspondence of the Foreign Ministers," pp. 1029–30. L. G. Otto, *Considérations sur la conduite du gouvernement américaine envers la France* (Princeton, 1945).

47. Mildred Stahl Fletcher, "Louisiana as a Factor in French Diplomacy from 1763 to 1800," *Mississippi Valley Historical Review*, 17 (1930), 367–77. See also E. Wilson Lyon, *Louisiana in French Diplomacy, 1795–1804* (Norman, Okla., 1934).

Except for the first few months following Adams' triumph, when he hoped that the President might be weaned away from the Hamiltonians,[48] Jefferson was obsessed with the belief that Adams sought a war with France and an alliance with Britain. He overlooked Adams' honest efforts to patch up the strained relations with France, and he never recognized Hamilton's desire to avoid war at this time.[49] What stuck in his mind was the President's call for stronger military defenses after news reached America of the rejection of Charles Cotesworth Pinckney as Minister and of ensuing depredations against American commerce.[50]

Although the Vice-President realized that France had made a mistake in rejecting Pinckney, he excused the action on the grounds that she had been the injured party in Franco-American relations ever since Jay's Treaty.[51] He threw all the blame for France's truculence upon the eagerness of his own government to precipitate a war between the two countries.[52] Sincerely worried about Federalist intentions, Jefferson also had the welfare of his party as an incentive to faithfulness to the one country that could serve the Republicans as Britain served the Federalists. Small wonder, then, that Talleyrand, the Minister of Foreign Affairs, was tempted to extort bribes from a new

48. Adet, Paine, and Madison concurred with TJ in the first months after the election. Adams, they thought, might be friendly to France if he fell under the influence of the Vice-President. TJ to Madison, January 22, 1797, L&B, *9*, 367–68; Adet to Minister of Foreign Affairs, March 10, 1797, Turner, "Correspondence of the French Ministers," pp. 993–94; Madison to TJ, December 19, 1796, *Writings of James Madison, 6*, 300–01; Paine to TJ, April 1, 1797, Jefferson Papers (L.C.), *101*.

49. Conversations with Adams, March 2, 1797, TJ, "Anas," L&B, *1*, 415. Hamilton to Pickering, Secretary of State, May 11, 1797, *The Works of Alexander Hamilton, 10*, 262. He wanted an American "Jacobin"—but not TJ or Madison—to convince France of America's peaceful intentions.

50. Adams' message to Congress, May 16, 1797, in J. D. Richardson, ed., *A Compilation of the Messages and Papers of the Presidents*, 1899–1902 (10 vols. Washington, 1899–1902), *1*, 233–38.

51. TJ to Thomas Pinckney, May 29, 1797, L&B, *9*, 390.

52. TJ to French Strother, June 8, 1797, ibid., *9*, 396; TJ to Aaron Burr, June 17, 1797, ibid., *9*, 400–01.

American peace mission in return for a settlement which France was just as anxious as the United States to effect.

This scheme—the so-called XYZ affair—was a mistake that should have been avoided. France in 1797 had already decided to end the friction between the two countries in order to prevent the Americans from joining the British in invading Louisiana, and she should have used the new peace mission as an opportunity to make amends for the insult to Pinckney in 1796. But Talleyrand was apparently so confident of the loyalty and power of the French partisans in America that he hoped to profit financially from the discomfiture of the Federalist envoys. As long as the Americans feared that France was seeking war, they could pay for the privilege of being left at peace. Consequently the envoys were met not by the government officials who usually greeted newly arrived diplomats but by three private emissaries and friends of Talleyrand—the anonymous X, Y, and Z—who informed them that the United States might secure a reconciliation with the help of a loan to the French government and a *douceur* to the Directors.

Although this proposition by blackmail enraged two of the commissioners, John Marshall and C. C. Pinckney, their wrath did not immediately daunt the French. One of the XYZ had the insolence to anticipate and reject their objections. Assuming that the envoys expected disclosure of the overtures to unite their countrymen against French demands, Y took pains to disabuse them of that hope. "You ought to know," he asserted, "that the diplomatic skill of France and the means she possesses in your country are sufficient to enable her, with the French party in America, to throw the blame which will attend the rupture of negotiations not on the federalists, as you term yourselves, but on the British party as France terms you."[53]

Marshall and Pinckney were willing, nevertheless, to risk the

53. Report of American mission to France, October 30, 1797, W. Lowrie and M. Clarke, eds., *American State Papers: Foreign Relations* (6 vols. Washington, D.C., 1832–59), 2, 164 (hereafter cited as ASP FR). Beveridge, *The Life of John Marshall*, 2, 278–79 (selected from Marshall's "Journal," October 30, 1797, pp. 25–26).

dangers suggested by the XYZ. They planned to spread the whole issue before the American public. Frightened by the possible consequences of their departure, Talleyrand prevented the more malleable Elbridge Gerry from joining his colleagues by holding out, alternately, threats of war and hopes of peace. It was too late; the news of the insult to national honor occasioned an outburst against France which surpassed the hostile reaction to Jay's Treaty.[54]

Jefferson's years of cooperation with France had led in 1798 to the destruction of most of the hopes he had nourished for himself and for his country. The Federalists, entrenched in power, were preparing, so it seemed to him, to set up a military dictatorship with the aid of martial law: Congress had ordered the suspension of commerce with France and had authorized American privateers to seize French ships suspected of preying on America's merchant fleet; the Alien Acts, aimed at Irish and French supporters of Republicanism, and the Sedition Act, designed to punish critics of Federalism, had as their goal the dissolution of his party. All these calamities that emerged from the XYZ affair were not sufficient to raise doubts in his mind about the wisdom of his policy toward France. Instead of attributing his misfortunes to the mistakes of France or of his own judgment, he attributed them to a Federalist conspiracy concocted by Hamilton and the British to destroy the republican institutions of the United States.[55]

Although the ambitions of French imperialists made a mockery of Jefferson's friendship with France, the reasons for his faith rested upon a higher moral plane than mere political expediency and upon a higher rational plane than unreasoning fear of Federalism. He believed that the Directory represented a return to the pristine virtues of the early Revolution, and he

54. Marshall Smelser, "The Federalist Period as an Age of Passion," *American Quarterly, 10* (Winter, 1958), 409–12.

55. TJ to Madison, May 31, 1798, L&B, *10*, 41. TJ to Thomas Mann Randolph, April 12, 1798, Jefferson Papers (L.C.), *103;* TJ to J. W. Eppes, April 11, 1798, Jefferson Papers (University of Virginia).

had apparently good evidence to justify this belief. In the first
year of his retirement he had heard about the fate of his unfortunate Girondist friends at the hands of demagogues like
Robespierre, who had seized control of the Convention with
the help of the Paris mobs.[56] By suppressing the Terrorists the
Directory appeared to have saved the Revolution and to have
provided safeguards in the Constitution of 1795 against future
anarchy.[57]

James Monroe, Jefferson's chief correspondent in France
from 1794 to 1797, facilitated the transfer of his affections from
the Girondists to the Directory by molding his impressions of
events in Europe. The men who in turn influenced Monroe
were moderate republicans, veterans for the most part of exile
and imprisonment under the Terror, who could be excused for
welcoming the arrival of a government that seemed to restrict
liberties to limits the people could absorb.[58] Fortified by this
knowledge, Jefferson was able to clear his conscience of the one
blot on the escutcheon of the Revolution. Although he had
earlier admitted that revolutions necessarily hurt the innocent
as well as the guilty,[59] the troubles of Lafayette, de Tessé, La
Rochefoucald, and other friends continued to disturb him.
But with the guillotining of Robespierre, the man he considered
the personification of whatever evil existed in the Revolution, he
could throw all the blame for their difficulties upon the excesses
of the Terrorists. He noted that the people responsible for
their personal misfortunes had been destroyed and that the new
government would fulfill the hopes of those who had wanted a

56. Monroe to TJ, September 7, 1794, *The Writings of James Monroe,*
2, 49.

57. Monroe to TJ, November 18, 1795, Jefferson Papers (L.C.), *99.* In this
letter he mentioned the defects of the new constitution, but added that it
was better than anything else of its kind in Europe.

58. Charles H. Van Duzer, "Contributions of the Ideologues to French
Revolutionary Thought," *Johns Hopkins University Studies in Historical
and Political Science,* 53 (Baltimore, 1935), 80–83.

59. The strongest statement was probably made in a letter to William
Short after he had heard of the September Massacres. TJ to Short, January
3, 1793, L&B, *9,* 9–10. See p. 51 above.

gradual reformation of society.[60] Fortunately for his peace of mind, Jefferson never came to grips with the painful fact that the Girondists had been no less responsible for the Terror than the most rabid Jacobin.

Jefferson's affection for the Constitution of 1795 was understandable in the light of the information he possessed on French affairs. What was less understandable was the inability or unwillingness of liberal Frenchmen who had direct or indirect contact with him to point out the imperialistic intentions of the Directory. Possibly Jefferson may have been too engrossed in his illusions or ambitions to profit from warnings, but at least they should have been forthcoming from sources other than reactionary *émigrés* whose testimony he would automatically discount.

Jefferson's contacts with Frenchmen were indeed limited during his retirement and Vice-Presidency, but he did maintain a correspondence with a few men he had known and respected in France who enjoyed personal prosperity under the Directory. These men, understanding the foreign policy of the regime and Jefferson's relation to it, willingly served the cause of the new imperialism despite its betrayal of revolutionary ideals and its threat to American security. One of them, Constantin, Comte de Volney, even visited Monticello during this period, and for two years enjoyed Jefferson's confidence as a fellow scholar and fellow republican.[61] At the same time he acted as an informal agent of Talleyrand, examining the possibilities of French colonization on the American continent.[62] Although he subsequently advised Talleyrand that French ambitions in Louisiana would antagonize Americans, his concern for American friendship was primarily to prevent potential American

60. TJ to Démeunier, April 29, 1795, Ford, *8*, 173–75. Démeunier, former editor of the *Encyclopédie méthodique*, was then an exile in London. It is noteworthy that TJ never made much distinction between the Thermidorians and the men of the Directory.

61. TJ invited him to Monticello in 1795 after Volney had renewed his acquaintance by sending him a copy of one of his scientific works. Gilbert Chinard, *Volney et l'Amérique* (Baltimore, 1923), pp. 34–35.

62. Ibid., p. 43.

resentment from interfering with France's designs before the Directory was prepared to strike.[63] Whether as a patriot and republican he had identified the interests of America with those of France it is impossible to say. Volney did not indicate, at any event, the ulterior motives of his visit to his Virginia friend.

Even friends who were themselves victims or opponents of the Directory served Jefferson no better than Volney, although it is unlikely that they misunderstood its ambitions. La Rochefoucald, a philosopher, aristocrat, and *émigré,* showed no indication of having enlightened Jefferson during his visit to Monticello in 1796.[64] Had he been really resentful of the Revolution, he would not have applauded as he did the retired statesman's actions on behalf of France at this time.[65] Patriotism seems to have been the reason for his loyalty to France if not to the Revolution. Lafayette, languishing in an Austrian prison, had made this position clear in 1793. The cause of liberty, he wrote to Thomas Pinckney, required the defeat of France's foreign enemies even though France herself was governed by tyrants.[66]

By failing to reveal to him the imperialistic intentions of the French government, Jefferson's friends helped to perpetuate his misconceptions about the Revolution itself. Had he understood the reasons behind the support of his candidacy in 1796, he might have been less distracted by fear of monarchy at home. But convinced that the Revolution was both sound and beneficial to America, he had permitted his ambitions and suspicions to betray his understanding of the balance of power. Consequently he was able to regard the invasion and defeat of Britain as a positive aid to American liberties,[67] and to accept rumors

63. Ibid., pp. 63, 81–82.

64. TJ to Colonel Hite, June 29, 1796, L&B, *9*, 345.

65. La Rochefoucald, *Travels, 2*, 524–26.

66. Lafayette to Thomas Pinckney, American Minister to Britain, July 4, 1793, *Mémoires, correspondance et manuscrits du Général Lafayette,* ed. H. Fournier Aîné (6 vols. Paris, 1838), *4*, 239–42.

67. In 1795 he had even talked of giving up his retirement to dine in London with Pichegru and "hail the dawn of liberty & republicanism in that island." TJ to W. B. Giles, April 27, 1795, Ford, *8*, 172.

of French interest in Louisiana as a warning to Federalists against going to war with France lest she avenge such a crime by taking Louisiana.[68]

Jefferson did not consciously play a role so much at variance with the original purpose of his personal alliance with France. He maintained that his actions served the interests of American democracy and security. Actually, they led by 1798 neither to peace nor to security, nor to a true friendship with France. He feared war with France although his collaboration with the French made such a catastrophe a possibility. He feared monarchy in America when the errors of his party repeatedly strengthened monarchical forces. He feared British victories at the very time when a British defeat would have exposed the United States to the malevolence of imperialist France. Some of his fears were valid, particularly those concerning the intentions of the monarchical wing of Federalism, but fear alone would not account for his behavior. Ignorance of France's goals, the psychology of a minority party leader, and the magnetic attraction of the Revolution also contributed to the shaping of his attitude toward France during these years.

68. TJ to Aaron Burr, June 17, 1797, L&B, *9*, 402–03.

5.

Jefferson the National Leader: 1799–1804

Through its appeal to the emotions, a revolution may dominate men's lives long after they have abandoned its tenets. This has been the fate in the twentieth century of the disillusioned Communists whose ideals have been mocked by the realities of Soviet imperialism. For them an admission of error in their judgment of Russia, or a renunciation of faith in Communist ideology has often failed to bring absolution from the influence of the Russian Revolution. A sense of guilt, it seems, has compelled men to denounce the good as well as the evil they once saw in the Revolution, and has induced them to transfer their missionary fervor to the cult of counterrevolution.

Jefferson's attitude toward France from 1798 to 1803 superficially resembled that of a disillusioned revolutionary. He who had upbraided violators of America's treaty with France gladly accepted a new agreement which permitted the United States to withdraw from the alliance; he who had upheld the principles of the Freedom of the Seas refused to join a league especially designed to uphold those principles; he who had regarded the military victories of France as the victories of American liberty was willing to threaten that same nation with an alliance with the British enemy. In short, Jefferson had adopted many of the policies of his Federalist opponents.

The change resulted from the loss of old illusions and the gain of new responsibilities, represented respectively by Napoleon Bonaparte's seizure of the government of France and by Jefferson's election to the Presidency of the United States. Upon assuming responsibility for the security of his country, Jefferson threw over his earlier faith in France in favor of a policy that weighed objectively America's connections with all foreign nations. The presence of a dictator in the land of the once-cherished Revolution, in turn, caused him to exhibit some of the hostility that is usually associated with the disappointed revolutionary.

Jefferson escaped this category because he lacked the dogmatic temper and immovability of principle of the cultists. He was essentially a pragmatist in revolution, believing in the potential ability of all peoples to achieve political liberty but only after they have been trained in the habits of free men. Having held this view of the French Revolution ten years before and having never consciously surrendered it, he was able to regard the Revolution's failure as the fault of the people that embraced it and not of the goals it sought. Far from blaming the rise of Bonaparte upon the evils of revolution, he looked upon his dictatorship merely as evidence that France had not heeded his plea for moderation in 1789. In fact, the regime of Bonaparte helped to conceal from Jefferson the threat to America's security contained in the foreign policies of the various revolutionary governments, since the American President did not learn the facts of French imperialism until the dictator brought them to his attention. Thenceforth Jefferson associated French aggression in America with Bonaparte rather than with the men who had laid the groundwork for Bonaparte's program. When he opposed France, he was not acting the part of a lover betrayed; he was the leader of his people, protecting them from a foreign nation that was hostile to America's interests.

In the fall of 1798 Jefferson observed few portents to warn him of the circumstances which in a few years were to make France his enemy and Federalist policy his own. Even had they been more discernible, his obsession with the malevolent ambitions of the Federalists might have prevented his noticing the most overt manifestations of France's imperialism. The only rays of light piercing the dark clouds of destruction which he saw hanging over America's future came from his confidence in the American people's abhorrence of Federalism's arbitrary authority and from his belief in France's sincere desire to avoid war with the United States.[1]

While Americans were growing restive under pressure of the Alien and Sedition Acts, Talleyrand, on the other side of the Atlantic, seemed to have been vindicating Jefferson's faith in the peaceful disposition of France toward his country. Realizing the disastrous effects that the XYZ affair might have upon French plans for Louisiana, the French Foreign Minister sought to convince the few Americans remaining in France that his government was anxious for peace. As Elbridge Gerry was preparing to leave for home, the Directory announced that French privateers operating in the West Indies would cease molesting American vessels.[2] Talleyrand next turned to Fulwar Skipwith, United States Consul General in Paris, with the news that the Directory would raise the embargo on American vessels in French ports and would release imprisoned seamen.[3]

It is understandable that such powerful Federalists as Rufus King, United States Minister to England, and Timothy Pickering, Secretary of State, doubted the sincerity of Talleyrand and preferred to regard his attempts at reconciliation as another French trick.[4] Their experience with the diplomacy of the Revolution had taught them caution. Moreover, the High Federalists now had no interest in a reconciliation. A solution of the Franco-American imbroglio would only invigorate their political enemies and sabotage their own plan for collaborating with the British in an attack upon Louisiana and the Floridas.[5]

1. TJ to John W. Eppes, February 7, 1799, Jefferson Papers (University of Virginia). TJ to Nicholas Lewis, January 30, 1799, L&B, *10*, 89.

2. Decree of Directory, July 31, 1798, ASP FR, 2, 222–23.

3. Talleyrand to Skipwith, August 6, 1798, ibid., 2, 227–28. These provocative decrees had been part of France's retaliation against Jay's Treaty.

4. King to Pickering, September 3, 1798, in Charles R. King, ed., *The Life and Correspondence of Rufus King* (6 vols. New York, 1894–1900), 2, 405–06; Pickering to King, November 7, 1798, ibid., 2, 459.

5. Arthur B. Darling, *Our Rising Empire* (New Haven, 1940), pp. 321–22. John C. Miller, *The Federalist Era, 1789–1801* (New York, 1960), p. 220.

Such were the feelings of the Hamiltonian Federalists who occupied the key positions in the Adams Cabinet. But these were not the feelings of the President, once his anger over the XYZ affair had cooled. He saw as clearly as did Jefferson the misfortune that war would bring to the United States, and he understood better than the Vice-President the folly of permitting the nation to fall into the orbit of any foreign power. He wanted peace with France on terms that respected the dignity and sovereignty of the United States.

Accordingly, Adams lent a sympathetic ear to reports of another American whom Talleyrand approached: William Vans Murray, a man for whose opinions the President had greater respect than he had for Skipwith's or even Gerry's.[6] Murray, American Minister to the Netherlands, after much reflection informed the President that the overtures which Talleyrand made through Pichon, Secretary of the French Legation at The Hague, were sincere.[7] Adams then submitted Talleyrand's subsequent letter of appeasement to the Senate on February 18, 1799, along with the announcement of Murray's appointment as Minister Plenipotentiary to France.[8]

By producing a schism between Adams and the Hamiltonians, this action set in motion a chain of events that culminated in Jefferson's election to the Presidency two years later.[9] The Hamiltonians in the Cabinet were shocked by this announcement, for they had been anticipating a final break with France. Their efforts to frustrate this mission led eventually to their ouster. Adams, to be sure, succeeded in sending the mission to France over the objections of his Cabinet, and the increase in his

6. Gerry had exhausted the patience of his friend Adams through his behavior in the face of Talleyrand's blandishments and threats. As for Skipwith, he was a notorious Republican and unreliable as a source of information.

7. Murray to Adams, October 7, 1798, in C. F. Adams, ed., *The Works of John Adams* (10 vols. Boston, 1850–56), *8*, 688–90. Murray's feelings were shared by J. Q. Adams, the President's son and Minister to Prussia. S. F. Bemis, *John Quincy Adams and the Foundations of American Foreign Policy* (New York, 1949), pp. 99–100.

8. Richardson, *A Compilation of the Messages and Papers, 1*, 282–83.

9. See Stephen Kurtz, *The Presidency of John Adams: The Collapse of Federalism, 1795–1800* (Philadelphia, 1957), pp. 348 ff.

popularity in 1800 over 1796 suggests that the nation supported his peace efforts. But the price he paid for this victory was defeat for reelection in 1800, as the cleavage within the party manifested itself at the polls. The principal beneficiary of Adams' efforts to keep peace with France was the nation's security—and Jefferson.

The Vice-President foresaw no such happy conclusion to the Franco-American imbroglio when he first learned of the Murray mission. He dismissed it as a Federalist ruse to sidetrack Talleyrand's overtures, for he could not believe that it signalized a split in the ranks of his political opponents. When Adams added Oliver Ellsworth and Patrick Henry (soon to be replaced by W. R. Davie), Jefferson was convinced that there was a plot to parry "the overtures of France under the guise of a dignified acceptance of them." He expected the Federalist commissioners to delay and to sabotage the negotiations.[10] He needed all the perspicacity of his friends in Congress to help him exploit the breach, at this juncture.[11] With victory in sight, Jefferson and his party prepared to avoid the mistakes of 1796, and in so doing established a new relationship between the Republicans and the French. In the campaign of 1799 Jefferson avoided the appearance of identifying French victory in Europe with the survival of American institutions, so that Federalist pamphleteers would have no cause to damn him as they had in the past as an agent of French atheism and anarchy.[12] Possibly the lessons of experience may have had their influence upon this new spirit of independence. He expressed resentment in 1799

10. TJ to Madison, February 19, 1799, L&B, *10*, 112–13. TJ to T. M. Randolph, February 26, 1799, Jefferson Papers (L.C.), *105*.

11. Closer to political realities, John Nicholas, Republican leader in Congress, undertook immediately to defend Adams. T. H. Benton, ed., *Abridgement of the Debates of Congress from 1789 to 1856* (16 vols. New York, 1857), February 20, 1799, *2*, 362.

12. Vernon Stauffer, "New England and the Bavarian Illuminati," *Columbia University Studies in History, Economics and Public Law, 72* (New York, 1918), 283. According to Theodore Dwight, writing in the *Hartford Courant,* he was "the real Jacobin, the very child of *modern illuminatism,* the foe of man and the enemy of his country." TJ defended the *illuminati.* TJ to Madison, January 31, 1805, Ford, *9*, 108–10.

over the "atrocious proceedings of France" which gave the Federalists pretext for seizing power—forgetting his own support in the past of French depredations upon American commerce and French insults to American sovereignty. While the resentment was not clearly defined at this time, it did exist as a vague challenge to both the French and the Federalists. Its first consequence was merely Jefferson's realization that the security of his country lay, as George Washington and Alexander Hamilton had said, in the abjuring of political connections with all foreign powers.[13]

Whatever the original cause for the change may have been, the new turn in his relationship with France took a more positive form when Jefferson learned of the sudden fall of the Directory. A *coup d'état* on November 9, 1799, put an end to the life of that body, and established the Consulate under the personal direction of Napoleon Bonaparte, the thirty-year-old general whose exploits in Italy and Egypt Jefferson had earlier admired.[14] This upheaval was inevitably a shock to the political and philosophical sensibilities of the man whose personal liaison with France had rested upon the common ground of republicanism. Even if the autocracy of Bonaparte was no more a betrayal of republican spirit than the Directory's oligarchy had been, its appearance was more difficult to disguise. In accepting the fact that the French Revolution was dead, Jefferson facilitated his full independence of France.

From the very beginning of his connections with France, the interests of his country and later of his own career had established the principal links. Liquidation of the Revolution freed his mind for philosophical reflections upon the political capacities of the French people, a subject he really had not examined for ten years.[15] As soon as the character of Bonaparte's regime

13. TJ to Thomas Lomax, March 12, 1799, L&B, *10*, 124. Two years before his famous Inaugural Address, he had written in this letter: "Commerce with all nations, alliance with none, should be our motto."

14. TJ to Madison, June 15, 1797, ibid., *9*, 397; TJ to Nicholas Lewis, January 30, 1799, ibid., *10*, 91.

15. Reports of Bonaparte's coup were so garbled at first that TJ feared at one moment that he intended to restore the Bourbons and hoped at the

became clear, he noted that the French lacked the "habit of self-government," and that a military dictatorship might be the most suitable form of government for a people lacking the talents of Americans.[16]

As Jefferson opened his eyes to the myth of French republicanism, he recognized that the new ruler of France was a veritable despot, who accomplished by his *coup* exactly what Hamilton supposedly wished to do in the United States.[17] But if he had opened his eyes wide enough, he would not have been so content to view the situation in France with equanimity. As far as he was concerned, the new government, while hostile to the ideals of Americans, need not be at all hostile to the reestablishment of peaceful relations between the two countries. In fact, Oliver Wolcott, a leading Hamiltonian, claimed that the Republicans even based their election campaign of 1800 on the fiction that President Adams was carrying out the program of reconciliation too reluctantly.[18] Even after the rise of Bonaparte Jefferson was persuaded of the sincerity of France's peace efforts, while he was not at all satisfied with the work of the American peace negotiators. It seemed strange to the Republican presidential candidate that the public should have heard no word from the envoys in Paris when it was known that the French government was willing to present the Americans with a carte blanche at the conference table.[19]

Jefferson's reaction to the Convention of 1800 demonstrated more clearly than any other index the initial change in his

---

next that he intended merely to introduce a single executive system to France similar to that of the United States. TJ to Henry Innis, January 23, 1800, ibid., *10*, 145–46; TJ to Dr. William Wardlaw, January 28, 1800, Coolidge Jefferson Papers (Massachusetts Historical Society).

16. TJ to John Breckenridge, January 29, 1800, Ford, *9*, 106–07.

17. TJ to Dr. William Bache, February 2, 1800, Jefferson Papers (L.C.), *106*. TJ to T. M. Randolph, February 2, 1800, L&B, *10*, 151.

18. Oliver Wolcott, Jr., to Fisher Ames, December 29, 1799, in George Gibbs, *Memoirs of the Administrations of Washington and John Adams* (2 vols. New York, 1846), *2*, 313–14.

19. TJ to T. M. Randolph, May 7, 1800, Jefferson Papers (L.C.), *107;* TJ to Madison, September 17, 1800, Ford, *9*, 144.

attitude toward France caused by consciousness of his new authority and by the character of Bonaparte's regime. This Convention announced the abrogation of the old treaties with France, the polestar of his foreign policy, and yet it evoked no protest from him. Although he did describe it as a "bungling negotiation," he was not objecting to the nullification of the old alliance; he was expressing his fear that some provisions of the Convention might compromise Anglo-American relations![20] The articles committing the United States to upholding the liberal principles of neutral rights were now unwelcome on the grounds that Great Britain might consider the Convention a repudiation of Jay's Treaty, which he had opposed so vigorously during the Administrations of his Federalist predecessors. But like the American Commissioners at Paris, Jefferson was willing to accept the unpleasant features of the agreement in order to escape the burdensome entanglement. As Vice-President he cast the deciding vote that prevented the President's enemies in the Senate from relegating discussion of the Convention to secret session and probable rejection.[21]

On the eve of his succession to the Presidency Jefferson assumed Adams' policy of seeking the preservation of American liberties through abstention from Europe's quarrels. Had Adams failed to win his fight against the Hamiltonians, who were enraged at the Convention's omission of indemnities for France's spoliation, the new President would have carried it to a successful conclusion after he took office.[22] Neither man suspected the hostile designs of France, Jefferson far less than Adams. The former hoped to remain a friend of France as long as the friendship did not demand any binding ties and did not interfere with America's amity with other nations. As spokes-

20. TJ to Madison, December 19, 1800, L&B, *10*, 185. Darling (*Our Rising Empire*, p. 385) suggests, however, that he objected to the Convention because it failed to challenge Jay's Treaty. He adduces no evidence to substantiate this interpretation of TJ's statement.

21. TJ to Caesar Rodney, December 21, 1800, Ford, *9*, 160; *The Aurora and General Advertiser*, December 23, 1800, reported TJ's action.

22. TJ to Colonel John Holmes, January 24, 1801, Ford, *9*, 172.

man for an entire nation, not merely for an opposition party, Jefferson was anxious to defer to public opinion which "is unequivocally understood to be that we shall haul off from European politics, have no political engagements with them, nor intermeddle in the smallest degree with anything which may entangle us in their quarrels."[23] Such was the credo of his famous Inaugural Address and the key to his new relationship with France.

Although Jefferson the President had announced his contempt for France's new political structure and then renounced America's alliance with that nation, his actions had not made him an enemy of France. Despite his intention of removing the United States from any participation in European affairs, his conception of the balance of power in Europe had not changed; Great Britain was still the major threat to America's security, and France's resistance was essentially a service to his country's interests. The new President did not know that the instrument that was to separate the United States from Europe—the Franco-American Convention of 1800—helped to make French imperialism a greater threat to the young republic than the more familiar British imperialism. He took up the reins of office handicapped by his misinterpretation of the significance of Bonaparte both to the balance of power and to the destiny of his own nation.

Napoleon Bonaparte was a far more dangerous enemy to the United States than the relatively inefficient body he had deposed. Like the Directory, he wanted to avoid arousing American suspicions while France was completing negotiations with Spain for the retrocession of Louisiana. This was a main purpose of his reconciliation with the United States; but it was not enough for the ambitious First Consul. He also wanted to exploit the American peace mission to further his war with Great Britain. American support for the principle of freedom of the seas would help him weld together the maritime powers

23. TJ to Stephen Sayre, February 16, 1801, Jefferson Papers (L.C.), *109*.

of Europe into an anti-British League of Armed Neutrality.[24]

What Bonaparte sought from the United States was a treaty that would uphold the liberal interpretation of neutral rights—particularly free ships, free goods, and a restricted contraband list—so that the small naval powers of northern Europe would have the necessary motive for joining a League of Armed Neutrality against British sea power. By this treaty a generous France would show herself to be a true friend of the rights of nonbelligerents, and the United States would be accessory to such a league: an ally in principle at least in the eyes of the participating powers.[25] Thus the Franco-American Convention of Morfontaine, signed on September 30, 1800, served a twofold purpose for Bonaparte: the advancement of united action among the northern neutrals and the removal of the danger of American interference in French plans for the New World. As if to crown his triumph, his representatives in Spain signed the secret Treaty of San Ildefonso, whereby Spain ceded Louisiana to France, one day after the Convention with the United States had been concluded.

Instead of worrying about Jefferson's discovering his duplicity, Bonaparte sounded out the possibilities of inducing the President to bring the United States into the League of Armed

---

24. Among American statesmen only Hamilton claimed that the Convention "plays into the hands of France, by the precedent of those principles of navigation which she is at this moment desirous of making the basis of a league of the northern powers against England." Hamilton to Theodore Sedgwick, December 12, 1800, *The Works of Alexander Hamilton, 10,* 397. Yet Hamilton, like the more moderate Federalists and like TJ himself, considered the Convention to be less harmful than other possible solutions. See Darling, *Our Rising Empire,* p. 379.

25. Charles Lebrun, the Third Consul, sounded the keynote of France's ambitions at the signing of the Convention when he proposed the toast: "To the Union of America with the powers of the North for securing the freedom of the high seas." Gazette nationale; ou, le Moniteur universel, October 6, 1800, p. 14, quoted by George F. Hoar, "A Famous Fete," American Antiquarian Society, *Proceedings,* New Series, *12* (Worcester, Mass., 1898), 257. See also Arthur A. Richmond, "Napoleon and the Armed Neutrality of 1800: A Diplomatic Challenge to British Sea Power," *Royal Service Institution Journal, 104* (1959), 1–9.

Neutrality.[26] The delicate Louisiana issue did not inhibit him since he had no intention of revealing news of its transfer until French troops had occupied the territory.[27] That day would come after Britain had been defeated and after the League had outlived its usefulness. In the meantime, Jefferson's reputation as an *idéologue* suggested that he might be receptive to the proposals of Thomas Paine and Joel Barlow, two prominent Americans in Paris who were intimates of the French intelligentsia. Either by coincidence or by direction of French officials, they had chosen the week in which the Convention of Morfontaine was signed to suggest to their old friend that the United States join with the European powers in checking British aggression on the seas.[28] If men like Volney and Destutt de Tracy, Du Pont and Lafayette, as well as Barlow and Paine, could succumb to Bonaparte's charms, their transatlantic colleague should be no more difficult to conquer. Jefferson's acceptance of nomination in November 1801 to the Class of Moral and Political Science of the National Institute seemed to bestow a Presidential blessing upon France under the Consulate.

Bonaparte appeared to many of the French friends of America as one of themselves—a liberal in politics, a student of science, an advocate of revolution through reform. As evidence of his qualifications as a man of progressive ideas, he was a member of the National Institute and had frequently shown favor to scientists and men of letters during the years he led armies in Italy and Egypt. Consequently, it required little self-deception for these *idéologues*[29] to regard his seizure of power as the

26. Pichon to the Minister of Foreign Affairs, May 14, 1801, AAE CP E-U, *53*, 115–18; Pichon to Minister of Foreign Affairs, July 23, 1801, ibid., *53*, 177–84.

27. Pichon to Minister of Foreign Affairs, December 1, 1801, ibid., *53*, 433–36vo. It was Pichon's duty to assure TJ that France had given up all designs upon Louisiana.

28. Paine to TJ, October 1 and October 4, 1800, Jefferson Papers (L.C.), *107*; Barlow to TJ, October 3, 1800, ibid., *107*.

29. *Idéologie* was the name coined by de Tracy in 1802 for the philosophical movement based largely on the sensationalistic theory of knowledge. Denoting no particular group, it encompassed most of the philosophy and

rescue of liberty from the corrupt hands of the Directory at a moment when the country was in danger.

The General himself made no effort to disillusion them, for he needed the support of respectable republicans.[30] Nor did their illusions fade immediately. Even the most prominent liberals had become too closely identified with the Constitution that legitimized Bonaparte's usurpation to make a repudiation an easy matter. Volney, Destutt de Tracy, and Emmanuel Joseph, Comte de Sièyes, representing the radical republican, limited monarchical, and moderate republican wings of the Revolution respectively, had seats in Bonaparte's Senate. Even those who could not regard Bonaparte as a republican considered him the heir of the Revolution, remedying with his strength the evils of the Directory. Lafayette, who admitted that the First Consul had overthrown the Republic, assured Jefferson of Bonaparte's good will toward the United States. He too was in debt to the dictator. The First Consul gave him no office, but he did give him back his freedom after long years of prison and exile.[31]

Neither Bonaparte nor Jefferson's French friends had any knowledge of the President's new views of France. First reports from America seemed to support the First Consul's expectations. The reservations which Jefferson had expressed about the French dictatorship had been largely confined to intimates; few could detect the changes in his attitude during the first days of his Administration. At the inaugural dinner, thirty of the one hundred and fifty guests were Frenchmen. The arrival of Louis Pichon, the French Chargé d'Affaires after the restoration of Franco-American diplomatic relations, was the

---

leaders of the Revolution in its fold, with the exception of Rousseau and the Terrorists. The Revolution sought by them was based on reason and reform. The United States was their model, and TJ their teacher.

30. Echeverria, *Mirage in the West*, p. 227.

31. Lafayette to TJ, February 10, 1800, Gilbert Chinard, ed., *The Letters of Lafayette and Jefferson* (Baltimore, 1929), p. 210; Lafayette to TJ, June 21, 1801, ibid., p. 213.

occasion for a warm official greeting; and in exchange Jefferson appointed one of France's oldest friends, Robert R. Livingston, to be the new American Minister to France.[32]

Through the accounts of Pichon, Bonaparte soon learned of the changes in Jefferson's attitude toward France. Basically friendly to America's republican aspirations, the French Minister accurately reported the new mood of the victorious Republicans. But he did not understand the reasons for the changes. The picture of the President which he drew from a series of interviews revealed none of Jefferson's revulsion against Bonapartism or his rationalizations for isolationism. Jefferson, in Pichon's eyes, was essentially the same man he had been in 1796, changed only to the extent that various considerations prevented him from exhibiting his friendship in the same manner as in the past.

The considerations which restricted the President's freedom of action in Pichon's view took two forms. The first was Jefferson's fear of exposing himself to Federalist attacks by joining France in any sort of common cause. The chances of America's rallying to the Armed Neutrality were therefore slight. Pichon was convinced that the best that France could expect from Jefferson was his good wishes for a successful conclusion to her struggle with Britain.[33] The other consideration noted by Pichon was Jefferson's resentment against France's double dealing in Louisiana, which might place America's friendly neutrality in jeopardy. Pichon's own knowledge of France's intentions in Louisiana led him to suspect every instance of American displeasure with France to be an indication that Jefferson had heard about France's acquisition of that territory. Although Pichon did not know whether the President believed his denial of the rumors which had been circulating in Washington, he

---

32. E. Wilson Lyon, "The Franco-American Convention of 1800," *Journal of Modern History, 12* (1940), 330. See also George Dangerfield, *Chancellor Robert R. Livingston of New York, 1746–1813* (New York, 1960), pp. 403–05.
33. Pichon to Minister of Foreign Affairs, May 14, 1801, AAE CP E-U, *53*, 115–18; Pichon to Minister of Foreign Affairs, July 23, 1801, ibid., *53*, 177–84.

did know that France would have to reckon with the wrath of an angry America when the rumors were verified.[34]

Pichon's interpretation of Jefferson's motives was erroneous. While it was true that a sensitivity to Federalist criticism and a concern for French imperial ambitions had their effect upon Jefferson's feelings for France, the French Chargé's impressions of his behavior were too much a reflection of his own apprehensions about the Louisiana problem. He did not understand that Jefferson's coolness toward France in the early period of his administration might have merely been evidence of his liberation from dependence upon France's military and ideological support. Granted that this liberation did produce some friction, it did not undermine the President's conviction that Britain was still America's chief enemy.[35] Although he declared his opposition to American participation in the League of Armed Neutrality, he still wished well to the efforts of any league which proposed to curb British power.[36] If Bonaparte was too optimistic in consigning the President to the category of the French *idéologues,* Pichon was too pessimistic in ascribing to Jefferson a complete knowledge of France's foreign policy.

Jefferson's rejection of the League of Armed Neutrality was not connected with the Louisiana issue; indeed it preceded even the rumors of the retrocession. It was part of the new status he had given France which made her just one more factor in the European balance of power.[37] If Bonaparte had no ally in

34. Pichon to Minister of Foreign Affairs, December 1, 1801, ibid., *53*, 433–36[vo].

35. TJ openly blamed the French for British aggressions against the United States. Their blunders had given aid and comfort to the British party in the United States. Pichon to Minister of Foreign Affairs, July 23, 1801, ibid., *53*, 177–84.

36. TJ to Thomas Paine, March 18, 1801, L&B, *10*, 223–24. The same answer was given to Joel Barlow. TJ to Barlow, March 14, 1801, ibid., p. 222.

37. Thornton, Secretary of British Legation in Washington, though skeptical of TJ's professions of friendship with Britain, thought he was sincerely free of attachments to France: "For *republican* France he might have felt some interest but that was long over, and there was assuredly nothing in the present Government of that country, which could naturally

Jefferson, he had at least no enemy in him as long as the President considered Britain the foremost threat to American security. Even the shock of the Louisiana revelations was not great enough to force Jefferson to reassess his understanding of the balance of power.

Despite Pichon's errors of judgment, the Frenchman's fear of Jefferson's and of America's reaction to France's repossession of Louisiana was not inordinate. When the truth of France's intentions became known, the former Francophile picked up every weapon at his disposal, not excluding the threat of an alliance with Britain, to express his disapproval of France. Louisiana appeared to have been the final element in the evolution of Jefferson from party chieftain to national leader. If Bonaparte's rise to power had given him doubts as to France's republicanism, the news about Louisiana had converted these doubts into fears, not for the future of French liberties but for the maintenance of American sovereignty.

Although France intended to conceal the fact of the Treaty of San Ildefonso until Louisiana had been fully secured, a secret involving such stakes was impossible to keep for long. Rumors of the transaction flew all over Europe, notably into the hands of the British enemy, who in turn relayed them to the Americans. Rufus King, the Federalist Minister to England, whom Jefferson was in no hurry to discharge,[38] reported in March, 1801 the news that a double disaster awaited the United States: cession of Louisiana and the Floridas to France, and negotiation of a Franco-British peace which would enable Bonaparte

---

incline him to show the smallest undue partiality to it at the expence of Great Britain or indeed of any other country." Thornton to Grenville, March 7, 1801, Public Record Office Transcripts in Library of Congress, Foreign Office 5, 32. Hereafter cited as PRO FO 5.

38. To alleviate worries about Britain's reaction to the Convention of Morfontaine, TJ needed a man in London whom the British would trust. Darling, *Our Rising Empire*, p. 398. See also Bradford Perkins, *The First Rapprochement: England and the United States, 1795–1805* (Philadelphia, 1955), p. 138.

to take advantage of his new property.[39] When these tidings reached the United States, Jefferson confided to his friends the ominous implications that the transfer of Louisiana would have for American security.[40]

From the moment he heard the news he began to wrestle with the problem of living next door to a new neighbor in control of New Orleans. It was an unhappy prospect he faced, filled with opportunities for violence in the event the French attempted to build an empire in America. Even if they did not intend to violate American territory, their probable interference with American commerce on the Mississippi would drive the Westerners either to war or to desertion of the Union. The solution for the United States lay only in Jefferson's ability to thwart fulfillment of the agreement between Spain and France. Such was his object.

War with France was one solution to the problem of Louisiana, but it was an unpalatable response for the President, considering his distaste for the cost of maintaining a large military establishment and considering his fear of a military caste which would thrive on war. The solution had to be a peaceable one, and in order to win time for working out a policy he appeared willing to accept the fiction that Louisiana was still Spanish. If he did not have to recognize the existence of a transfer, he would not have to take any immediate steps until France actually secured possession of the territory.[41] In

39. Rufus King to Secretary of State, March 29, 1801, Despatches, United States Department of State, *9*, in National Archives.

40. Madison acknowledged King's report about Louisiana and mentioned similar reports arriving from other quarters about the same time. Madison to King, June 15, 1801, *Writings of James Madison, 6,* 434–35. The King dispatch arrived May 29, 1801, and TJ's comments followed almost immediately. TJ to Monroe, May 26 and 29, 1801, Ford, *9,* 259–62. Mary P. Adams ("Jefferson's Reactions to the Treaty of San Ildefonso," *Journal of Southern History, 21* [May, 1955], 174–75) claims that TJ did not trust to chance or to diplomacy for solutions to his difficulties, but prepared the country for a military "showdown." The Lewis and Clark expedition in this light is seen as a "military reconnaissance."

41. In informing Claiborne of his appointment as Governor of the Mississippi Territory, TJ emphasized the importance of Louisiana's remaining in Spanish hands. TJ to William Claiborne, July 13, 1801, Ford, *9,* 274–75.

the meantime, it was conceivable that something could arise that would nullify the Franco-Spanish deal. Hence his annual message to Congress in the fall of 1801 contained no reference to the Louisiana problem. The President in that year had made every effort to maintain friendly ties with France even though it involved the acceptance of Bonaparte's conditions for the ratification of the Convention of 1800 and might require the reception of French envoys Laforest and Otto whom he considered to be anti-republican if not anti-American.[42]

By 1802 the melancholy observations of Robert Livingston on France's imperial plans induced Jefferson to announce not only his knowledge of the Treaty of San Ildefonso but also his opposition to it. Pichon reported the change. Shortly after the President had assured the French Minister of his faith in France's disclaimers about Louisiana, he began to hint at a rupture between the two countries that would take place as soon as war was resumed in Europe. To avoid this state of affairs, Jefferson suggested that France provide Americans with favorable commercial concessions on the Mississippi.[43] He had apparently decided to face the fact of French imperialism without waiting for French troops on American soil to rouse him to action.

The President's aim now was to persuade France by intimidation to give up her ambitions in America. The price of America's friendship would be more than economic favors from the new masters of Louisiana; France would have to cede New Orleans, the Floridas, all the territory that she received from Spain. If France should refuse his request, he predicted, she

42. TJ to Livingston, August 28, 1801, and March 16, 1802, ibid., *9*, 295 and 356. In the second letter, TJ retreated from the position of the first, particularly with respect to the French envoys. He "did not harbor a doubt that the disposition on that side of the water was as cordial, as I knew ours to be." This attitude may have been part of a design to avoid seeking evil so that he would not have to find any. His letters during this period, unlike Madison's, omitted references to Louisiana, and concentrated on neutral rights.

43. Pichon to Minister of Foreign Affairs, January 2, 1802, AAE CP E-U, *54*, 15–17[vo].

would lose the territory the moment the perennial troubles of Europe distracted her attention from the New World. France would be wiser to give up the land voluntarily and retain the good will of the United States. The alternative for Americans was an alliance with Britain. Dramatically, almost theatrically, Jefferson warned that "the day that France takes possession of N. Orleans, fixes the sentence which is to restrain her forever within her low-water mark. It seals the union of two nations, who in conjunction, can maintain exclusive possession of the ocean. From that moment we must marry ourselves to the British fleet and nation."[44]

The President wrote these often quoted words in a letter to the American Minister to France for the beneficial effect he hoped they would have upon its bearer, Pierre Samuel Du Pont de Nemours, a distinguished physiocrat and a friend for almost twenty years. Although Du Pont was then a resident of the United States and was departing for France for what he thought would be only a brief stay, Jefferson saw an opportunity to exploit the economist's contacts with the French government by having him publicize the seriousness with which the United States regarded the Louisiana cession.[45] Lest the Livingston letter fail in its purpose, the President sent Du Pont a note in which he asked him to impress upon his fellow countrymen the importance of ceding all French territory in America, not just New Orleans.[46]

The unofficial emissary of America served faithfully the task which Jefferson had chosen for him, but he did not accept it until his pride as a Frenchman had been appeased. The President's tactics, he thought, would antagonize rather than intimidate the French. It would be better for the United States to help the French win Canada in exchange for the surrender of Louisiana, for such a gesture would permit the arrangement to appear reciprocal. If this plan were impossible, he advised,

44. TJ to Robert Livingston, April 18, 1802, L&B, *10*, 311–16.
45. TJ to Livingston, May 5, 1802, Jefferson Papers (L.C.), *123*.
46. TJ to Du Pont, April 25, 1802, L&B, *10*, 316–19.

Jefferson should offer a reasonable price for the territory at issue, in language that would not offend Bonaparte.[47]

While appreciating the spirit of friendship evidenced by Du Pont's reply to his suggestion, the President was not at all pleased with the idea of purchasing Louisiana. He had anticipated France's compliance with his wishes on the strength of his threats and on the hope of new conflicts in Europe.[48] Only when his alternatives seemed to be purchase or war did Jefferson turn to the Du Pont plan. The world situation in general and his political fortunes in particular allowed no other solution in 1802. Abroad, the Peace of Amiens had been made in the very month in which he had made overtures to Du Pont, and Rufus King reported that Britain, despite her interest in the disposition of Louisiana, would not bring the Louisiana question into her negotiations with France. Edward Thornton, the British Chargé d'Affaires in Washington, even suggested that if the French should occupy Louisiana, the British would have greater influence over a frightened United States.[49] Bonaparte was therefore free to complete his plans for the occupation of the territory. At home, the President had to contend with the rising anger of the Westerners over the prospect of having their rights of deposit in New Orleans taken away by the new rulers of the Mississippi. Pinckney's Treaty with Spain in 1795 had given the United States the right to navigate the Mississippi from its source to the sea, and to deposit its goods at New Orleans for transshipment to ocean-going vessels. Spain suspended this right in October, 1802, and France was immediately blamed for the affront. Federalists were able to use Western discontent to embarrass the administration by demanding re-

47. Du Pont to TJ, April 30, 1802, Gilbert Chinard, ed., *The Correspondence of Jefferson and Du Pont de Nemours* (Baltimore, 1931), pp. 48–54.

48. TJ to Livingston, May 5, 1802, Jefferson Papers (L.C.), *123*. TJ to Joseph Priestley, January 29, 1804, L&B, *10*, 446–47.

49. King to Livingston, January 16, 1802, *The Life and Correspondence of Rufus King*, *4*, 57–59. Thornton to Lord Hawkesbury, May 30, 1803, PRO FO 5, *38*.

dress from France and posing as the new champions of the West.[50]

The President responded to these challenges by employing a weapon that his predecessors had used successfully a few years before: a special mission empowered to settle a special problem. He chose James Monroe to be Minister Plenipotentiary and Envoy Extraordinary to France to help Livingston win Louisiana from the French. Jay's mission in 1794 had postponed Republican attacks until a treaty with Britain had been made; Monroe, a popular figure in the West, might have the same success, not only in silencing the Federalists but also in dampening the ardor of the West for war. Jefferson authorized the two envoys to purchase New Orleans and the Floridas alone for a price slightly less than what was finally paid for the entire Louisiana territory, and to guarantee if necessary the rest of the territory to the French. Should France appear hostile, they were to open talks with the British about the possibility of cooperating in a joint venture against French Louisiana.[51]

Thus Jefferson seemed to have completed over a period of four years the process of detaching himself from France by going beyond the policy of isolation to consider a British alliance long advocated by the Hamiltonians. Such an extreme course is characteristic of the ex-revolutionary of every era, who, finding his love betrayed, will seek any means to destroy the former object of his affections. The President's behavior, however, was not an emotional by-product of hatred for France. At no time did he express personal anger toward that country, or, conversely, extend a sincere welcome to Britain as a defender of liberty. His flamboyant talk of a British alliance was only a gambit of international politics in which he hoped to use Britain to intimidate France, for he never seriously considered an alliance with Britain as a real possibility. Britain remained

50. George Cabot and Fisher Ames to King, April 3, 1802, *The Life and Correspondence of Rufus King, 4*, 105–06.

51. Henry Adams, *History of the United States of America During the Administration of Jefferson and Madison* (9 vols. New York, 1890), *2*, 2.

the traditional enemy in the eyes of the President and of the Secretary of State, for whom Britain's ambitions in the West, transgressions on the seas, and possible stipulations for the price of support overbalanced the transitory threat of France.[52]

Inasmuch as France never completed her empire in America, there can be no certainty as to the extent to which Jefferson might have gone to counter the moves of Bonaparte. During the difficult days of 1802 his fears often dented the armor of confidence he had built out of hopes that the troubles of the Old World would in some way prove to be his salvation. On such occasions he would be convinced that France would force the United States into the arms of Britain, and so he took pleasure in noting every manifestation of friendship on the part of the British.[53] But generally Jefferson's dallying with Britain was so half-hearted and so palpably self-seeking that Thornton, with whom he attempted to ingratiate himself in gloomy moments, distrusted his sudden appreciation of British merits and claimed that he seemed to tax "his imagination to supply the deficiency of his feeling."[54] Thornton was right. When Jefferson's mood of despair lifted, he trusted in the intervention of a *deus ex machina*—war in Europe, revolution in the West Indies, or financial difficulties in France—to make France see the light and to keep his country out of the clutches of Britain. Months before he had seen any of his hopes realized, the President railed against those Americans who would have the United States take immediate action on Louisiana. Nothing but dire

52. TJ to Livingston, October 10, 1802, L&B, *10*, 335. In instructing them to contact the British if their mission failed, Madison made it clear that a connection with Great Britain was a last resort. Madison to Livingston and Monroe, April 18, 1803, *Writings of James Madison*, 7, 39–41.

53. There were groups in Britain which regarded France's acquisition of Louisiana as an opportunity for an Anglo-American rapprochement. British intervention, they felt, would make the United States appreciate the usefulness of the mother country. This argument is found in George Orr, *The Possession of Louisiana by the French Considered as it Affects the Interests of Those Nations More Intimately Concerned, viz. Great Britain, America, Spain and Portugal* (London, 1803). TJ to Rufus King, July 13, 1802, L&B, *10*, 329–30.

54. Thornton to Grenville, March 4, 1801, PRO FO 5, 32.

necessity, he asserted, could force the country out of neutrality and into the orbit of Britain.[55] And such a crisis looked distant as reports began coming in about the restoration of American rights of deposit in New Orleans, the imminence of war in Europe, and the difficulties that Leclerc's French armies were having in occupying the island of Santo Domingo.[56] The President's willingness to guarantee Louisiana to France as well as his talk of a British alliance must be weighed against his knowledge that the future of the territory irrevocably belonged to the rising West and against his conviction that British services should never be used to help obtain it.

When all Louisiana and not just New Orleans fell into the hands of the surprised envoys in May 1803, the event took place in the manner that Jefferson had predicted. Bonaparte had to sacrifice his imperial ambitions in the New World, temporarily at least, before the altar of a new war in Europe. Since British sea power would have prevented him from occupying his American empire, he deemed it advisable to sell the entire territory to the United States, despite the dubious legality of such a transaction, and receive in return funds to carry on his European ventures. Other explanations for the First Consul's actions are available. George Dangerfield has recently pointed out that failure in Santo Domingo made war in Europe inevitable: Bonaparte needed a new arena in which to recoup his losses.[57] Whatever may have been the ultimate factor in the decision, Jefferson had a right to feel that he had won complete success. He had vindicated not only the policy of non-entanglement advocated by Washington and Adams but also the assumption he had made as Secretary of State: America's advantage from Europe's distress.

55. TJ to William Dunbar, March 3, 1803, Jefferson Papers (L.C.), *130*.

56. TJ to Governor McKain [McKean], June 14, 1802, ibid., *124;* TJ to Lewis Harview, April 22, 1803, ibid., *131:* TJ to John Bacon, April 30, 1803, Ford, *9,* 464; TJ to Gideon Granger, May 8, 1803, ibid., *9,* 465–66; TJ to Governor Claiborne, May 24, 1803, L&B, *10,* 390–91.

57. H. Adams, *History of the United States, 2,* 25 ff.; Dangerfield, *Robert R. Livingston,* p. 375.

Although Jefferson from 1798 to 1803 appeared to have cut most of the bonds that had formerly linked his emotions and his activities favorably to the French nation, his experiences did not make him either a political or an ideological Francophobe. He did not wake up to French imperialism until the Directory had fallen, and when it finally made an impression upon him, it was associated with Bonaparte and not with the Revolution. With the Revolution destroyed, it seemed that Jefferson had forgotten his own vigorous championship of France a few years earlier. He bore no grudge against the people who betrayed his faith.

Jefferson the President had taken up the view of France he had held as Minister to that country, when he had urged cautious reform so that she might more effectively serve as a buffer protecting the United States from Britain. He was therefore disappointed but not particularly surprised or disturbed by the mere fact of a firm dictatorship. Whatever the government, French power could still serve the purposes of American policy as long as the United States did not allow itself to become involved in Bonaparte's European conflicts. Even the intrusion of the Louisiana issue did not basically affect Jefferson's interpretation of the balance of power which he had formulated years before. While Louisiana in French hands made France the chief threat to America in 1802, she was only a temporary menace to American sovereignty with which he could cope by trusting in Europe's propensity for wars and in his own skill in diplomacy. Britain, on the other hand, was a permanent and far more dangerous adversary. But for the moment, the contribution of the new Anglo-French war to the Louisiana Purchase permitted him to consider Britain and France each "as a necessary instrument to hold in check the disposition of the other to tyrannize over other nations."[58]

58. TJ to Monroe, January 8, 1804, Ford, *10*, 67–68.

6.

The President versus the Emperor of the French: 1804–1809

Professor W. Stull Holt once compared the young American Republic of 1800 to a jackal living off the spoils it steals from more powerful animals diverted by fights among themselves.[1] The United States picked up Louisiana in this manner, but like the jackal she ran the risk of becoming involved in European struggles.

Jefferson would have appreciated this view of the republic. Indeed, he had used a similar metaphor that placed even greater stress upon the precarious position of the United States in relation to the balance of power in Europe: "Tremendous times in Europe! How mighty this battle of lions and tigers! With what sensations should the common herd of cattle look on it? With no partialities certainly. If they can so far worry one another as to destroy their power of tyrannizing, the one over the earth, the other the waters, the world may perhaps enjoy peace, till they recruit again."[2] Nevertheless, he expected that the United States would not only survive the strife but would "fatten on the follies of the old [nations]" by winning new territories and new concessions from their wars.[3]

As minister to France, secretary of state, vice-president, and president, Jefferson was in a position not only to formulate a

1. W. Stull Holt, "Uncle Sam as Deer, Jackal, and Lion; or, The United States in Power Politics," *Pacific Spectator*, *3* (January, 1949), 47–48.

2. TJ to Benjamin Rush, October 4, 1803, L&B, *10*, 422.

3. TJ to Edward Rutledge, July 4, 1790, Boyd, *16*, 601.

concept of a balance of power to be expressed in this kind of metaphor, but also to put into effect or at least to influence policy decisions based on his understanding of the balance of power in Europe. For him and for many of his colleagues that balance represented the equilibrium achieved by the distribution of economic, political, and military strength of the world among several great powers in such a way that no one of them was strong enough to destroy the others and thereby menace the security of nonbelligerents. Even if the balance was never exact, the rapacious powers of Europe could sufficiently check each other to assure to smaller nations the maximum degree of peace and stability possible in a world governed by force. A further result of this deadlock was the possibility that a small neutral, such as the United States, might enhance its power and prestige by expanding its borders at the expense of the preoccupied nations of the Old World.

It is not surprising that the fortuitous success of his Louisiana negotiations should have made Jefferson discontent with the role of the "common herd" and willing to compete more boldly in the arena of William Pitt and Napoleon Bonaparte. Profiting from the struggles of Britain and France was a legitimate function of his policy only so long as it kept the risks to national security within reasonable bounds. By pitting Britain against France and France against Spain to preserve and extend his original profits in Louisiana, the President jeopardized both profits and security.

At the same time, he revealed a view of the balance of power in Europe which accepted with equanimity the prospect of a French victory at the moment that England was fighting a lonely battle to maintain the balance on the Continent. The course of war after Britain's naval triumph at Trafalgar and after France's victory at Austerlitz in 1805 turned almost exclusively to economic warfare, which in turn affected the commerce of neutral nations. Britain, deprived of allies on the Continent, and France, lacking sea power, had no other means of coming to grips with each other. In this situation, no matter how offensive England's behavior toward the United States, the great naval power was fighting a defensive war against an aggressor bent on world conquest: Jefferson never accepted this fact.

Napoleon Bonaparte—Emperor of the French after 1804— exploiting the President's cupidity to further France's commercial war against Britain, succeeded in his maneuvers against the United States in 1807 where he had failed in 1801. But it was not entirely trickery that brought the United States into the periphery of the Continental System. In Jefferson's estimation France continued to present fewer evils for the United States than did her British rival. France's supremacy on land rendered the United States safer from attack than did Britain's control of the seas; if he had to favor one of the two powers, France would usually be his choice. Even the possibility of total victory for the French tyrant did not jar the American president from his complacency. He preferred to deal with a present evil than with a "future hypothetical one." He was willing to leave the future to the "chapter of accidents" which had hitherto been so kind to the fortunes of the United States.[4]

Shortly after the satisfactory solution of the Louisiana problem, Monroe unwittingly gave the President an opportunity to fully express his motives in cultivating foreign friendships. While in France as special envoy Monroe noticed that Jefferson's correspondence with influential Frenchmen had produced a good effect during his mission. He suggested, therefore, that relations with literary and philosophic personages be continued and nourished, especially with those connected with the National Institute. He was convinced that the National Institute was the most powerful organization in France outside the executive circle itself.[5]

If Jefferson's reply to these observations was somewhat didactic in tone, it was not because he thought that Monroe had mis-

4. TJ to Thomas Leiper, August 21, 1807, Ford, *10*, 483–84.

5. Monroe to TJ, September 20, 1802, Jefferson Papers (L.C.), *134*. TJ himself had been elected to the National Institute in 1801. See Comte de Franqueville, *Le premier siècle de l'institut de France* (Paris, 1895), *2*, 55.

understood or overestimated the role of the intellectual in imperial France. He merely regarded the advice as gratuitous, since he had examined long before and put into operation just such a project with reference to British as well as to French intellectuals. He had consciously made use of his relations with Lafayette and Du Pont when he was minister to France. More recently, he pointed out to Monroe, he had been writing freely to men of the stature of Volney, Du Pont, and Pierre Jean George Cabanis "on subjects of literature, and to a certain degree on politics, respecting however their personal opinions, and their situation so as not to compromit them were a letter intercepted." Most of his suggestions were of the kind that "would do us good if known to their governments, and, as probably as not, are communicated to them." The President was confident that he was able to make "private friendships instrumental to the public good by inspiring a confidence which is denied to public, and official communications."[6] It is no coincidence that both Destutt de Tracy and Du Pont were elected members of the American Philosophical Society during Jefferson's presidency of that organization.

After the fall of the Directory, Jefferson's respect for the judgment of his French friends weakened. It was never without reservation. His comments about them and attitude toward them became even more patronizing than in the past. The fact that most of them had embraced Bonaparte upon his accession to power led him to wonder if their views and principles were sufficiently advanced to permit their understanding of the free institutions of the United States.[7] Looking at the wreckage of the Revolution in 1800 and at the indecent eagerness with which the intelligentsia welcomed the young conqueror, the President showed his contempt for them by suggesting that the national character of the French was not suited to a republic and needed the ministrations of a dictator to prevent chaos.[8]

6. TJ to Monroe, January 8, 1804, Ford, *10,* 60–61.
7. TJ to T. M. Randolph, February 2, 1800, L&B, *10,* 150.
8. TJ to Volney, April 20, 1802, Jefferson Papers (L.C.), *122;* TJ to Mme. de Corny, January 31, 1803, Gilbert Chinard, ed., *Trois amitiés*

Aside from their putative influence in Paris, the French philosophers had little to offer Jefferson. He read only such samplings of their works as Say, Cabanis, and Du Pont periodically sent for his inspection. Even Destutt de Tracy, for whom Jefferson performed literary services without expectation of political compensation, did not plant any new ideas in the President's mind.[9] What he admired in these men, particularly in Destutt de Tracy, was their skill in expressing his own ideas, not their ability to teach philosophical or political principles. Whenever their ideas corroborated his own thoughts about politics or economics or morality, he treated them with full respect. Should they omit points which he considered essential, or should they assert concepts which differed from his own, he would label their work too "metaphysical" or too "European."[10] Jefferson already had shown these prejudices when he was minister to France, but not until his Presidency and retirement did he fully express his independence from European thought.

His affection for and gratitude to his comrades remained undiminished. He sincerely urged Lafayette and Du Pont to return to the United States so that he might enjoy the pleasure of their company and benefit from their knowledge of scientific and philosophical matters. As inducements he considered offering Lafayette the governorship of Louisiana and wanted Du Pont to open an academy in New Orleans;[11] but these offers were not proofs of their influence over Jefferson—they were mere tokens of his friendship. President Jefferson accepted

---

françaises de Jefferson, d'après sa correspondance inédite avec madame de Brehan, de Tessé, et de Corny (Paris, 1927), p. 212; TJ to Cabanis, July 12, 1803, L&B, *10*, 405.

9. After his retirement, TJ personally translated Destutt de Tracy's *Treatise on Political Economy* from the unpublished French original and wrote a prospectus for it, praising the work.

10. TJ to J. B. Say, February 4, 1804, L&B, *11*, 3; TJ to Joseph Mulligan, April 6, 1816, ibid., *14*, 462. See Wiltse, *The Jeffersonian Tradition in American Democracy*, p. 51.

11. TJ to Lafayette, November 4, 1803, Chinard, ed., *The Letters of Lafayette and Jefferson*, pp. 225–26; TJ to William Claiborne, May 25, 1806, Chinard, ed., *The Correspondence of Jefferson and Du Pont de Nemours*, p. 98.

Du Pont's effusive congratulations over America's acquisition of fine French stock in Louisiana in the same spirit that an experienced teacher might listen to the ideas of a brilliant but callow student. Admitting these many fine qualities, he explained to Du Pont that the Creoles would not make good American citizens until they had learned the meaning of self-government.[12] All he would offer for the immediate future was as much liberty as the people could bear, a form of government which was not too different from that which he had advocated for the French themselves in 1789. Du Pont and Lafayette could be Jefferson's political advisers no more than the French people could be the political equals of Americans.

For all Jefferson's perceptiveness of weakness in even the most distinguished French thinkers, his tactics with the intelligentsia bore no fruit. If anyone gained an advantage from his relationship with these correspondents it was Bonaparte. The French philosophical liberals did not enjoy special favors from him; rather they became objects of imperial persecution once the Emperor no longer needed their services. He ridiculed them, deprived them of a free press and free speech, and drove many of them out of the country—all without losing the support of most of them.[13] The motives for their remarkable behavior were complex. They represented a belief among most liberals that Bonaparte's crimes, bad as they were, were preferable to the return of the Bourbons. At least he had brought to France liberal impulses, embodied in the equalization of taxes and the extension of education, and they hoped that in the long run these reforms would destroy his tyranny.[14] Bonaparte's greatest

12. Du Pont was appeased by TJ's reasoning but the Louisianans were not. They presented a memorial to Congress in 1804 indignantly complaining about the arbitrary executive and judicial powers vested in the Governor. Du Pont to TJ, May 12, 1803, ibid., p. 73; TJ to Du Pont, January 19, 1804, ibid., p. 81.

13. See Van Duzer, "Contributions of the Ideologues," pp. 151–63.

14. Lafayette lamented the fate of good liberals forced into exile, but thought that these "jolts and bars" would not disturb the liberal impulses given France by the United States. Lafayette to TJ, Chinard, ed., *The Letters of Lafayette and Jefferson*, p. 253.

hold on the intelligentsia was the power of patriotism. Whenever they became too disturbed about the shortcomings of the French government, they had only to look across the Channel and see the alternative of British conquest. Typically, Lafayette blamed Britain, not Bonaparte, for violating the Treaty of Amiens and renewing the war.[15]

That Bonaparte commanded the loyalty of these men even as he victimized them would not under ordinary circumstances have had a particularly adverse effect upon the United States. It would have meant merely that Jefferson's idea of using private friendships for public purposes did not succeed. But during Jefferson's second administration, at a time when he needed a clear understanding of the Emperor's purposes, the silence of the liberals was at least in part responsible for Jefferson's failure to realize the significance of Bonaparte's tyranny and helped to confirm the President's conviction that Britain was the primary threat to American security. Lafayette and Du Pont praised every project against Britain. When, earlier, the President had spoken of a possible connection with Britain prior to the purchase of Louisiana, Lafayette was more upset over such a possibility than he had been about the actuality of Bonaparte's tyranny. "Could I divest myself of my french feelings," he asserted, "I should still think it very dangerous for the United States to entangle themselves in any close connection with Great Britain."[16] Du Pont went even further with his advice. In his letters to Jefferson he made a point of urging him to seize Canada lest the British attack the United States from Canadian bases.[17] Although he never made specific mention of France's interest in America's relations with Canada, his repeated exhortations were in the interest of France's war effort. It was not surprising, therefore, that the steps leading to the embargo, which brought the United States into the

15. Lafayette to TJ, September 1, 1803, ibid., p. 224.
16. Lafayette to TJ, March 31, 1803, ibid., p. 218.
17. Du Pont to TJ, March 10, 1806, July 12, 1807, August 13, 1807, July 23, 1808, Chinard, ed., *The Correspondence of Jefferson and Du Pont de Nemours*, pp. 108, 112, 120, 128.

service of Bonaparte's Continental System, met with their heartiest approval, and few voices in France were raised warning the United States against entering the War of 1812.[18]

Responsibility for the President's actions in supporting the embargo and, after his retirement, in urging war rested in the final analysis upon his own judgment. Du Pont and Lafayette gave their opinions in good faith. They saw no conflict between the intentions of France and the interests of the United States. Lafayette, in particular, encouraged Jefferson to believe that Napoleon could be persuaded to understand the common interests of France and the United States and that men such as himself could push him along this path.

Abused by the Emperor, the *idéologues* looked all the more eagerly to Jefferson as their exemplar and to his administration as the embodiment of all their goals—limited government, equality before the law, free press. In short, the United States was the type of nation they had once hoped would emerge from the French Revolution or from Bonaparte's Consulate. Perhaps their continuing passion for America reflects their slim but still real hopes that close friendly ties between the two countries would result in the ultimate extension of some of the American virtues to France, even to a France under the Emperor. As a testament to their faith, they accepted the judgment that a British victory in the war would be a greater disaster to France and to the United States than the realization of Bonaparte's plans for world conquest.

Jefferson, for his part, was stimulated by their ardor and flattered by their attention. Besides, he shared their basic assumptions, even if he could see clearly their weaknesses. His error was in joining them in minimizing the evils of the Empire

---

18. Du Pont called the Embargo an act of courage. Du Pont to TJ, July 24, 1808, ibid., p. 135. Mme. de Staël was one of the few French liberals to urge TJ to take a stand against Napoleon during the War of 1812. In his reply, TJ deplored Napoleon's acts but declared Britain to be the greater threat to the United States. Mme. de Staël to TJ, November 10, 1812, Marie Kimball, "Unpublished Correspondence of Mme. de Staël with Thomas Jefferson," *North American Review, 208* (1918), 66–68; TJ to Mme de Staël, May 24, 1813, L&B, *13*, 237–45.

and in overestimating their influence in Bonaparte's government.

The President could not foresee the future in 1803. It sufficed for him that his program hitherto had more than met his expectations, and that the future seemed to offer more opportunities for the United States to win commercial advantages from the warring powers and further territorial concessions from hapless Spain. At last the time had come when, as Jefferson had predicted years before, the Spanish empire in America was ripe for picking. With the approval of Britain and France, the Florida and Texas boundaries of Louisiana should have been the first fruit, and there seemed at first to be no opposition to American ambitions from either belligerent. Britain's reaction to America's acquisition of Louisiana was far milder than Rufus King or Jefferson had anticipated. Far from showing resentment, Lord Hawkesbury expressed to the American minister in Britain his appreciation for the solicitude shown to British interests in the navigation of the Mississippi.[19] Talleyrand also contributed to Jefferson's mood of optimism by suggesting that the United States claim as much of Florida as Spain would permit.[20]

The prospects, therefore, seemed limitless, and not only to President Jefferson. In Paris both Livingston and Monroe saw an opportunity to extend American authority to the east bank of the Mississippi, and then to claim that West Florida was part of the Louisiana purchase even if neither the French nor the Spanish had realized it.[21] Should there be some technical difficulties in implementing this assertion, American claims against Spain for her depredations against American commerce

19. Hawkesbury to King, May 19, 1803, *The Life and Correspondence of Rufus King, 4,* 263.

20. Darling, *Our Rising Empire,* p. 509.

21. Dangerfield, *Robert R. Livingston,* p. 374; H. Adams, *History of the United States, 1,* 246. Irving Brant, *James Madison: Secretary of State, 1800–1809* (Indianapolis, 1953), p. 149, suggests, however, that the French "deliberately laid the ground" for a claim to West Florida.

should overcome legal disabilities.[22] Beyond West Florida lay the rest of Spain's possessions east of the Mississippi, and this too should fall to the United States by exercise of statecraft or of military pressure. The Mobile Act of 1804, with its tentative assumption that the territory west of the Perdido River was American, was merely the first step in the process of winning control of all the Floridas.

Although Jefferson had sent Monroe to Spain to secure that country's acceptance of his interpretation of the Louisiana boundaries, he expected and discounted Spanish objections. Spain's keen sense of injury over Bonaparte's betrayal of his promise not to alienate the territory and her unrealistic hope that the Louisiana purchase would disrupt the American Union both militated against an early settlement of the problem. Jefferson knew this and was not disturbed. "We shall certainly obtain the Floridas," he observed, "and all in good time."[23] That would be when Spain became involved in European wars.

But earlier successes in fact made him impatient. His new governor of Louisiana, William Claiborne, repeatedly suggested a simple and obvious course: seize the Floridas. But the President had a more attractive alternative, one that he had used before to advantage: exploit the quarrels of Europe. Pressure on France, the country that controlled the destiny of Spain, would provide the solution without war or bloodshed. The task did not seem too difficult, especially since the United States had many claims against France, including claims for damages done to American commerce by Spanish vessels under French orders. In Madrid, the French ambassador even appeared to take the initiative in supporting American boundary claims. Above all, as Monroe learned in Paris in 1804, as long as the Florida issue was essentially a matter of money, Jefferson was justified in his hopes for French mediation.[24] Monroe's optimism nurtured these hopes.

None of these expectations materialized. Talleyrand's hos-

22. H. Adams, *History of the United States*, *1*, 249.
23. TJ to John Breckenridge, August 12, 1803, L&B, *10*, 408.
24. H. Adams, *History of the United States*, 2, 292, 305–06.

tility, rarely concealed for long, now combined with Napoleon's own schemes for Spain to make clear to Americans by the end of 1804 that France would support none of their goals—neither reparations for Spanish spoliations, nor boundary rectifications, nor the cession of East Florida. In fact, Talleyrand now explicitly said that West Florida was not included in the Louisiana cession.[25] The French attitude, reflected in the instructions to General Louis Turreau, the new minister to the United States, was one of shock over American aggression toward their client.[26] This hostility was quickly reciprocated by Americans abroad who reported to the President that it had been Napoleon, and not Spain, who had closed the port of New Orleans to American commerce in 1802. [27]

Jefferson was not disturbed. He remained as optimistic as he had been in September, 1804, when he assured his Attorney General, Levi Lincoln, that "good humor and reason" would allay Spanish feelings about the Mobile Act.[28] His mood struck a notable contrast with those of his intimates: Monroe, at the scene in Spain and France, urged action in Florida and was willing to risk war with England, France, and Spain; Madison, sharing Jefferson's aims but not his sang-froid, sought no move that would threaten the status quo; and Gallatin, annoyed more than alarmed, doubted if Florida was worth the risks Jefferson apparently had in mind.[29] It seemed to his advisers that the President was prepared to advocate nothing less than an alliance with Great Britain, hitherto the permanent object of Republican fears.

Jefferson's means were less clear than his ends. Recognizing that France's support explained Spain's resistance to America's

25. Talleyrand to Napoleon, November 20, 1804, AAE CP E-U, 57, 393–97.
26. Talleyrand to Turreau, July 23, 1804, ibid., pp. 88–92vo.
27. Charles Pinckney to TJ, February 28, 1805, Jefferson Papers (L.C.), *147*; Jacob Wagner to TJ, July 29, 1805, ibid., *151*. Most likely, the initiative was wholly Spanish, a reprisal against American smuggling. See Dangerfield, *Robert R. Livingston*, p. 353.
28. TJ to Levi Lincoln, September 8, 1804, Ford, *10*, 103–04.
29. H. Adams, *History of the United States*, *3*, 48–49, 62–65.

demands, he was prepared in 1805 to bluff Napoleon out of his position, even as he had tried through Du Pont to bluff him out of New Orleans two years before. He would induce Napoleon to acquiesce by making him believe that the United States was not averse to war or to a military connection with England if necessary to protect the national interest. He asserted these threats so vigorously that Madison, if not Napoleon, took them seriously. It was all right, according to the Secretary of State, for the President to mention the possibility of increased friendliness between England and the United States, but language which included talk of a treaty and a provisional alliance was going too far.[30] Was it possible that Napoleon's intrigues in Spain had frightened Jefferson into a realization of the signficance of French imperialism?

Jefferson promptly cleared up all doubts about his flirtation with Britain. He even showed a little annoyance that an old friend, such as Madison was, should have misunderstood his intentions. Of all his advisers, the Secretary of State should have been the first to understand that he had no intention of bringing the United States into war or into an alliance. The treaty with Britain, he emphasized, was to be provisional, effective only "on the event of our being engaged in war with either France or Spain during the present war in Europe." This was unlikely, but even if it should come to pass, he would insist that Britain make important concessions on issues over which the two countries had quarreled in the past. The explanation completely mollified Madison, who knew as well as Jefferson that Britain would never fight a war to win boundary changes or new territories for the United States without exacting reciprocal advantages that Americans would not sanction.[31] All that Jefferson really wanted from talk of a treaty with Britain was that speculation about such a negotiation should spread to France and Spain, so that those two countries might hasten to settle boundary and indemnity claims.

30. Madison to TJ, August 20, 1805, Jefferson Papers (L.C.), 152.
31. TJ to Madison, August 27, 1805, L&B, *11*, 87; Madison to TJ, September 1, 1805, Jefferson Papers (L.C.), *152*.

The President's bluff was never tested if only because Britain sabotaged his project before he could get it under way. The *Essex* decision of the British Prize Courts of July, 1805 subjected to capture French colonial goods which had been sent to the United States for reexportation to France. The British Admiralty judge, Sir William Grant, declared that the payment of drawbacks on those goods nullified their neutralization, thereby striking the first of a series of blows against the lucrative neutral trade Americans had enjoyed in transshipping French colonial products to the mother country. When news of this decision reached America, it raised such a clamor that the President had to forego further consideration of even a provisional accommodation with Britain.[32]

But even without the intrusion of the *Essex* affair there is no evidence that Jefferson ever wished to go beyond annoying France by posturing as a partner of England in an entente if not in a formal alliance. He welcomed the extension of war on the Continent when France attacked Austria as a respite from pressure, as an occasion to renew negotiations with greater prospects of success than before. He seemed to revert with relief to the caution of Gallatin who, during the rumors of alliance and treaty with Britain, had urged suspension of all diplomatic efforts without, however, abandoning any ground.[33] Napoleon's engagement in what should have been a protracted Austrian campaign could change France's attitude toward the United States. Perhaps the Emperor's restated support of the rights of neutrals was a step in this direction.[34]

At any event, French absorption in Europe proved to Jefferson the wisdom of his restraint over Santo Domingo. When Paine had urged him to use American influence in the confused affairs of that former French colony, Jefferson expressed alarm.

32. Secretary of the Navy Jacob Crowninshield reported national indignation over British interpretation of the doctrine of original voyage. Crowninshield to TJ, September 11, 1805, ibid., *152;* TJ to W. C. Nicholas, October 25, 1805, Ford, *10,* 179.

33. Gallatin to TJ, August 17, 1805, Jefferson Papers (L.C.), *152;* TJ to Gallatin, October 23, 1805, ibid., *153.*

34. TJ to Paine, March 25, 1806, Ford, *10,* 246–47.

"Our policy must be to follow events, to keep our lead-line ahead, sounding as we go, and steer accordingly."³⁵ A year later, the President could point out to John Armstrong, Minister to France, the wisdom of his moderation. By barring American shipping from Santo Domingo, despite opposition of American merchants and his Federalist opponents, he was doing more than appeasing Southern fears of the Negro domain in the Caribbean; he was giving France an earnest of American good will, and he expected a return for this behavior.³⁶

Had gratitude been a quality possessed by Napoleon, his decisive victory over Austria at Austerlitz would probably have muted it anyway. Fortunately for Jefferson's peace of mind, the armory of his statecraft was stocked with more than one weapon. In 1802 he had simultaneously loosed blandishments, threats, and money, and they appeared to have succeeded. If he had failed to beguile either France or Britain, he might still win his objectives by a combination of the other two weapons. Military action was always a possibility, and its proponents included Monroe and Armstrong who both urged him to send troops to the Sabine River and occupy Texas. Robert Smith, former Secretary of the Navy, advised the President to send gunboats to New Orleans, and to build battleships to carry out attacks against Spanish territory.³⁷ Jefferson's annual message to the Congress at the end of 1805 spoke of force in Florida and the active defense of free citizens on the Mississippi. But in a secret message he asked the Congress for two million dollars to purchase the territory. He concealed this pacific move beneath the show of martial ardor, so that European diplomatists would not suspect a change in tactics. He would win once again the fruits of war without fighting one. To Henry Adams, his attempt to play Talleyrand "resembled an amateur imitating Talma and Garrick."³⁸

35. Paine to TJ, January 1, 1805, Jefferson Papers (L.C.), *146;* TJ to Paine, January 15, 1806, ibid.

36. TJ to Armstrong, February 14, 1806, Ford, *10,* 230–31.

37. Robert Smith to TJ, September 10, 1805, Jefferson Papers (L.C.), *152.*

38. H. Adams, *History of the United States, 3,* 115; Leonard D. White, *The Jeffersonians: A Study in Administrative History* (New York, 1951), pp. 142–43.

This maneuver failed ignominiously because the situation in Europe and in America was not the same as the one that had led to the winning of Louisiana three years earlier. First of all, the secret proposals to France put him in the position of paying for the same land he had already claimed belonged to the United States; secondly, the money he was willing to pay for the Floridas was not sufficient to meet France's designs; and, thirdly, the plan precipitated a dangerous schism in the ranks of the Republicans. John Randolph, Jefferson's leader in the House, used the Florida purchase proposals as a vehicle to attack the President's control of the party. Its immediate effect was to estrange Gallatin from Randolph, to pit Randolph against Madison, Jefferson's heir apparent, and to strain relations between Monroe and Jefferson, as Randolph gathered support for the former's presidential ambitions in 1808. Ironically, Randolph's champion against the pro-French administration was himself the most francophilic of the Jefferson circle, according to the observations of Virginia newspapers.[39] Thus, Florida became a focus for discontent with administration policy, although the idea of a third party implicit in the term Quid never truly emerged from Randolph's assaults.[40]

Randolph failed in his efforts to destroy the President's project, but part of the cost of victory was the impetus it gave to Federalist charges of French domination of the Administration.[41] More serious was the emptiness of the victory itself. Even before the Two Millions Act was signed on February 13, 1806, the war which Jefferson had welcomed as a means of softening Napoleon had ended.

To contemporary European observers, as well as to historians today, Jefferson's attempts to bend Europe's power to America's advantage looked ludicrous. Britain and France both understood that his bellicosity was merely an empty gesture

39. Joseph I. Shulim, *The Old Dominion and Napoleon: A Study in American Opinion* (New York, 1952), p. 103.

40. Noble E. Cunningham, "Who Were the Quids?" *Mississippi Valley Historical Review*, 50 (1963), 261–63.

41. S. E. Morison, *The Life and Letters of Harrison Gray Otis, Federalist, 1765–1848* (2 vols. Boston, 1913), *1*, 275.

and that beneath his bravado was neither the will nor the ability to fight for his objectives. His clumsy experiments at playing off one power against the other had convinced them that they had nothing to fear from any move the United States might threaten to make. Turreau reported that Jefferson would avoid war under any condition, no matter how much he blustered, since he counted upon Europe's weakness to secure his goals. Admitting his admirable qualities as a private citizen, he claimed that as a statesman he lacked the boldness, the energy, and even the dignity of a true leader.[42]

Both powers easily victimized the hapless young republic. In the knowledge that they could discount American opposition to their policies, the British after their great victory at Trafalgar used their mastery of the seas to destroy America's neutral trade. The Emperor showed even less consideration for the United States. America's weakness convinced him of the value of keeping alive the friction between Spain and the United States which would serve his grand scheme of world conquest. Napoleon continued to dangle the Floridas before Jefferson's eyes to make the United States an agent of his imperialism. Jefferson's embargo was his reward.

As the European war developed into a duel between the Colossus of the Land and the Leviathan of the Sea, the plight of the United States as a neutral worsened. France's military might having conquered every enemy on land and Britain's sea power having swept the oceans clear of all her foes, the two belligerents turned their attention to the role of neutrals. Britain concentrated her major efforts after 1805 on blockade of Napoleon's Europe, while France, unable to retaliate on the seas, countered by establishing the Continental System which sought Britain's downfall through deprivation of her European markets for manufactured goods, thus reinforcing the British blockade. The chief sufferers in a struggle of this sort were in-

42. Turreau to Talleyrand, January 20, 1806, AAE CP E-U, *59*, 21–30; Turreau to Talleyrand, May 10, 1806, ibid., *59*, 140–51.

evitably the ships, commerce, and sovereignty of neutral nations, and no matter what the policy of the President had been in this situation the United States would have undergone severe tribulations. A clear understanding of the balance of power, nevertheless, might have enabled Jefferson to avoid, or at least lighten, the difficulties the nation had to suffer during these years.

The changing nature of the war did affect the President. Without deflating the confidence he had in his ability to make Europe's wars serve America's interests, it deflected his diplomacy from Spain to problems of neutral rights, the prosperity of American commerce, and even the survival of his country. The state of public opinion in 1806 and 1807 made some action imperative. Britain's and France's war of decree and counterdecree was in reality a war against neutrals. Each Napoleonic decree and British order in council damaged American rights, and Jefferson had no choice but to fight back.

The deliberate insolence of Britain's behavior toward his country was an important factor in inducing Jefferson to choose a weapon that accommodated the war aims of Napoleon. After the death of Charles Fox, Britain met every one of Jefferson's peace gestures—the threat of a nonimportation act as well as the blandishment of a special treaty mission—with the same contempt. Crowning insult to American pride was Britain's handling of the impressment issue. One of his major reasons for sending Monroe, along with William Pinkney, to London in 1806 was to make a treaty that would end the kidnapping of American sailors from American ships on the grounds of their being British deserters.[43] If Britain had acted with moderation, she might have softened American feeling. Although the President shared Gallatin's objection to Madison's plan of surrendering voluntarily any British deserter in American service, their reason was a fear for American morale rather than injured pride. Even after strong rebuffs, Jefferson was willing to con-

---

43. See Bradford Perkins, *Prologue to War: England and the United States, 1805-1812* (Berkeley and Los Angeles, 1961), pp. 101–40.

tinue negotiations that would find a satisfactory compromise.[44] Britain, however, abandoned all caution, and the *Chesapeake* incident, in which the British ship, *Leopard,* hailed, fired upon, and boarded the American frigate, *Chesapeake,* on June 22, 1807, in Virginia waters, was the result. The British killed three men in the process, and abducted four, only one of whom was an Englishman.

Jefferson was as shaken by this enormity as any of his countrymen. He immediately summoned his Cabinet to consider measures of retaliation. Angry as the President was, his behavior was not that of a man carried away by emotional impulse, for an obvious reply to such an insult was war. Instead he ordered all armed vessels of Great Britain to depart from American waters.[45] He talked about war in his correspondence with Du Pont and Lafayette, and even in conversations with the French minister Turreau.[46] Nevertheless, Jefferson was more interested in "peaceful means of redressing injustice" than in war, and he eagerly listened to reports that Admiral Berkeley had disavowed the act of the *Leopard* and that British officers ashore in Norfolk had shown only peaceful dispositions toward the United States.[47] He declared that he wanted to give the offender an opportunity to make amends for the crime, to grant American merchants time to bring their ships and property back to American soil in the event of war, and, finally, to allow the question of war to be determined by the proper constitutional authority, the Congress.[48]

44. TJ, "Anas," L&B, *1,* 446–47. Cabinet meeting, February 2, 1807. Gallatin to TJ, April 13, 1807, Jefferson Papers (L.C.), *166.* TJ to Madison, April 21, 1807, L&B, *11,* 193.

45. Proclamation of July 2, 1807, Richardson, *A Compilation of the Messages and Papers, 1,* 423.

46. TJ to Du Pont, July 14, 1807, Chinard, ed., *The Correspondence of Jefferson and Du Pont de Nemours,* p. 116; TJ to Lafayette, July 14, 1807, L&B, *11,* 279; Turreau to Talleyrand, July 18, 1807, AAE CP E-U, *60,* 166–71. When TJ failed to take a strong stand with the British, Turreau bitterly gave up all hope for a people "who have no idea of glory, grandeur, and justice." Turreau to Talleyrand, September 4, 1807, ibid., *60,* 199–201.

47. William Tatham to TJ, July 1 and July 3, 1807, Jefferson Papers (L.C.), *167.*

48. TJ to George Clinton, July 6, 1807, ibid., *11,* 258. Henry Adams claimed

President Jefferson did not avoid war with Britain this time because of any belief that Britain was fighting America's battle against Napoleonic imperialism; in the President's mind, Britain's action in the *Chesapeake* affair was only an extreme example of the malice she had always borne the United States. He avoided war because, as he conceived, he had a better instrument with which to strike Britain: an embargo cutting off American commerce nominally with all of Europe. It was actually directed against the British Isles, since the British navy had already effectively stifled trade with all countries under Napoleon's control. This scheme was obviously more than just an answer to the *Chesapeake* affront. Jefferson might have had satisfaction from the British if he had been willing to accept an apology and amends for that crime, but in asking for amends he insisted as well upon the abolishment of impressment itself.[49] The incident between the *Leopard* and the *Chesapeake* was merely the occasion that forced him to choose this particular weapon against the enemy, not the reason for his choice.

The embargo came at the time it did because America's position had degenerated so rapidly after the *Chesapeake* affair that an audacious action—war or its equivalent—was imperative. In the period from June to December, 1807, when the act went into effect, Jefferson's meek reply to the British atrocity had encouraged the belligerents to continue their attacks on neutral rights. The result was the rejection of American demands for redress, the enforcement of the Berlin Decree, the promise of more rigorous impressment policies, and the orders in council of November, 1807, forcing American ships into British ports to pay for permission to trade with the Continent.

The embargo was not altogether a new policy for Jefferson. To some degree it was the realization of an old dream that Jefferson shared with other Founding Fathers: the isolation of the United States from the evils of the Old World. As such, it

---

that TJ would not have delayed calling the Congress into emergency session if he had really wanted war. H. Adams, *History of the United States, 4,* 34–35.

49. Ibid., *4,* 39–40.

was a measure that fitted easily into a pattern of behavior which he periodically had advocated for the "common herd" when endangered by the jungle world of international politics. Inasmuch as Britain and France had virtually banned American commerce from the seas, the embargo could be a face-saving means of giving their decrees the force of American law, and thus remove a source of conflict with the belligerents. This conception of the embargo was more in consonance with the ideal role of a small nation than were other considerations that motivated the President and the Secretary of State at this time: territorial and pecuniary advantages that might be derived from Britain's vulnerability to commercial retaliation.[50] Instead of regarding the embargo as primarily a refuge, Jefferson envisioned it as a panacea which would protect American property, force the belligerents to revoke their decrees, strike a blow for neutral rights, and even help to win the Floridas.

In the embargo message, Jefferson made a point of emphasizing the new construction of the Berlin Decree, as if the embargo were directed against France. Three out of the four documents attached to the message dealt with French violations of American neutrality. This impression was deliberately misleading. Jefferson knew well that its first effect would be to give teeth to the Non-Importation Act against Britain that had gone into effect eight days before the embargo. The President believed that if Britain were deprived of her food imports and also of raw materials for her industry, powerful British manufacturers would force the government to yield to American demands.[51] One of Jefferson's aims was to strike a hard blow at

50. TJ to G. K. van Hogendorp, October 13, 1785, L&B, 5, 183. Louis M. Sears seems to have regarded the embargo as a natural outgrowth of TJ's philosophy of life and not as a measure of opportunism, as Adams emphasized (Sears, *Jefferson and the Embargo* [Durham, N.C., 1927], pp. 1–2). Sears gives too great a role to TJ's pacifism, however, as a cause of the embargo. See also Brant, *James Madison: Secretary of State,* pp. 397–403, and White, *The Jeffersonians,* pp. 423–44.

51. In November 1807, TJ thought that if no wheat reached England by May, she would be starved into submission. W. E. Dodd, "Napoleon Breaks Thomas Jefferson," *American Mercury, 5* (1925), 311; Schuyler D. Hoslett, "Jefferson and England: The Embargo as a Measure of Coercion," *Ameri-*

Britain without committing his country to war and without bringing upon himself the charge of being a French agent. It cannot be denied that Jefferson was fully aware that the embargo constituted a service to Napoleon. He more than admitted knowledge that the embargo would not hurt France; he went out of his way to convince Turreau, who had charged him with placing France on the same footing with Britain, that the United States had no intention of treating both countries alike. "The embargo which appears to hit France and Britain equally," the President told the French minister, "is for a fact more prejudicial to the latter than the other by reason of a greater number of colonies which England possesses and their inferiority in local resources."[52] France, unlike Britain, was reasonably self-sufficient; the supplies she needed from without could be obtained for the most part from her continental tributaries. While the Federalists saw through Jefferson's public pose of equal treatment of the belligerents and immediately sought political advantage from his aid to Napoleon, they were mistaken in looking upon his actions as evidence of a belief that France was more friendly to the United States than was Britain, or that French violation of neutral rights was less hateful.

Jefferson was aware of the deceit and malevolence of Napoleon. He confessed that it was "mortifying that we should be forced to wish success to Bonaparte, and to look to his victories as our salvation."[53] The alternative seemed to be British domination, and France was unwittingly serving the cause of neutral rights. "I never expected to be under the necessity of wishing success to Buonaparte. But the English being equally tyrannical at sea as he is on land and that tyranny bearing on us in every

cana, 34 (1940), 39. TJ was gratified in the following spring to learn of complaints in Liverpool about the embargo's effects. TJ to Caesar A. Rodney, April 24, 1808, L&B, *12*, 36.

52. Turreau to Champagny, June 28, 1808, AAE CP E-U, *61*, 166–77. Turreau was reporting this information to Talleyrand's successor as Minister of Foreign Affairs.

53. TJ to Col. John Taylor, August 1, 1807, L&B, *11*, 305.

point of either honor or interest, I say, 'down with England'
and as for what Buonaparte is then to do with us, let us trust
to the chapter of accidents. I cannot, with the Anglomen, prefer
a certain present evil to a future hypothetical one."[54]

Because he was convinced that France was not an immediate
threat to America's security, Jefferson saw the embargo as an
offensive as well as a defensive weapon. Remembering Napoleon's pose as a champion of neutral rights, he pretended to
offer the embargo as America's blow in behalf of maritime
liberty[55] and also as America's equivalent of joining the Continental System.[56] In return, Jefferson hoped Napoleon would
force Spain to cede the Floridas and rectify the western boundary—a hope based on the Emperor's promise to Armstrong, the
minister to France, that if the United States made an alliance
with France against Britain, Jefferson would be free to inter-
vene in Spanish America.[57] Thus the embargo would teach
England that her crimes were costly, and it would inveigle
France into working for America's territorial aggrandizement,
all without the cost of one American life.[58] If a French victory
resulted, the Atlantic Ocean would prevent Napoleon from
attacking the United States, if some other obstacle in the "chapter of accidents" did not stop him first.

In this dangerous diplomatic game Napoleon outplayed
Jefferson. The Embargo Act, intended as a fair exchange for

54. TJ expressed these sentiments in reply to the suggestion that Bonaparte was possibly Providence's instrument for punishing the crimes of
kings. Leiper to TJ, August 20, 1807, Jefferson Papers (L.C.), *170;* TJ to
Leiper, August 21, 1807, Ford, *10,* 483–84.

55. TJ to Paine, March 26, 1806, ibid., *10,* 247; TJ to Alexander I, April 19,
1806, ibid., 249–51; TJ to William Duane, July 20, 1807, L&B, *11,* 292; TJ
to Paine, October 9, 1807, ibid., *11,* 378.

56. John Armstrong to Champagny, February 8, 1808, AAE CP E-U, *61,*
36–36ʳᵒ; Turreau to Champagny, June 28, 1808, ibid., *61,* 166–77.

57. Armstrong to Champagny, February 4 and 8, 1808, ibid., *61,* 32–33 and
36–36ʳᵒ. Armstrong's hopes for Florida depended upon a promise the French
made, before they knew of the embargo, in return for an alliance.

58. I. J. Cox's "Pan-American Policy of Jefferson and Wilkinson," *Mississippi Valley Historical Review, 1* (1914), 212, claims that TJ's desire for
Florida influenced his whole relationship with Bonaparte.

the Floridas, in effect made American an ally in the Continental System without securing one square foot of Florida soil in return. Instead, the Emperor's price kept rising: repeal of all restrictions against French commerce, the right to plunder American ships, and ultimate involvement in the war with Britain. As a first step, he ordered the Bayonne Decree in April, 1808, permitting confiscation of any American ship found in European harbors, on the spurious grounds that he was aiding enforcement of the embargo. When Americans complained about the maritime restrictions or about France's procrastination over Florida, they were told that Jefferson himself had stated the embargo was aimed at France, and hence the Emperor's measures represented a natural reprisal. In the same facetious manner French officials refused to listen to American designs on Florida, because Spanish law prevented the king from alienating any of his territory.[59]

Jefferson naturally and openly resented this cavalier treatment. But his retaliation seemed petty and inadequate in view of the provocations. He annoyed Turreau by his talks with British envoys in Washington, by his refusal to capture French deserters in the United States, and by the strict accountability to which he held any ship leaving an American port for France on a special mission.[60] Aside from these pinpricks, the President did little to assert America's independence of French foreign policy, certainly nothing to hurt France's war effort. To the very end of his administration he maintained that Britain's sea power made her the greater danger to the United States; the Spanish uprising against French domination in 1808 served only to convince him that France would never carry out a program of overseas aggression. Indeed, Jefferson even speculated about France's difficulties in Spain making this the proper time to take action against Spanish America.[61] His deep-rooted fear of British power, combined with the temptations offered by

59. Turreau to Champagny, June 28, 1808, AAE CP E-U, *61*, 166–77.
60. TJ to Madison, May 31, 1808, L&B, *12*, 70; TJ to Gallatin, July 4, 1808, ibid., *12*, 79; TJ to Madison, August 12, 1808, ibid., 126.
61. TJ to Henry Dearborn, August 12, 1808, ibid., *12*, 125.

cooperation with France, had induced him to throw over his official policy of encouraging a deadlock between the "lions and the tigers" and to risk instead a final French victory.

Repeal of the Embargo Act coincided with the expiration of Jefferson's term as President of the United States. Britain, sure that the embargo would damage America more than herself, stubbornly persisted in executing her maritime policies and was rewarded by the opening of Spanish markets in time to offset loss of American trade. France, considering the United States as just another satellite, saw no reason for thanking Jefferson. In fact, Napoleon's minister in Washington welcomed the prospect of revocation in the expectation that the next American step would be war with Britain.[62] As for the United States, the embargo did severe damage to agriculture and commerce and brought unpopularity to Jefferson's administration. The loopholes in the act, widespread violations of its provisions, and the threat of secession in New England all contributed to the failure of the program.

Jefferson's despair over the fate of the embargo and of his career was not justified by the facts. During his two terms in office he had assumed responsibility for doubling the territory of the United States and had succeeded in the even more formidable task of keeping his country out of Europe's wars. The embargo itself, had it lasted longer, might have forced concessions from Britain.[63] The unhappiness of his last days as President was due in part to an overestimation of America's coercive powers and, in larger measure, to circumstances beyond his control. A major difficulty with the embargo was not in its composition or in its general purposes but in the special reasons Jefferson had for adopting it. Designed in part as an instrument to punish Britain, its failure portended a shift to less peaceful means of achieving this objective. In leading directly to the War of 1812, the embargo policy pointed up the flaws in Jefferson's understanding of the balance of power in Europe.

62. Turreau to Champagny, July 3, 1809, AAE CP E-U, *61*, 238–47[vo].
63. Sears, *Jefferson and the Embargo*, p. 318.

Fortunately, he did not have to pay for his assumption that the United States might safely favor the cause of France over that of Britain. He failed to understand that the dynamic imperialism of Napoleon's tyranny could not have left the United States at peace after it had humbled Britain. While the latter was undoubtedly hostile to America's growth, she waged war essentially as an unwilling defendant against the expansionism of France. The ultimate downfall of Napoleon probably saved Jefferson and his successors from having France rather than Britain as a neighbor in Canada.

7.

Reflections on France in Jefferson's Old Age: 1809–1826

Jefferson's retirement from public life in 1809 was permanent and unaccompanied by the mental reservations that had marked his retirement from the Department of State in 1793. He was sixty-seven years old. Forty of those years had been devoted to the service of his country. He had achieved in this period the highest office that his country could bestow upon any man, but in winning this success he had had to accept the bitter knowledge that the people had repudiated him in his last days as President. He was glad to return to Monticello, to the joy of combining the agrarian with the contemplative life.

As his long career had brought both success and failure, so his long retirement of seventeen years brought its share of happiness and sorrow, perhaps in the same proportion. Few situations in his life were more humiliating than his unsuccessful appeal to the legislature of Virginia for funds to save his estate from bankruptcy. Having long neglected his private affairs, he had need of the financial aid of fellow citizens who remembered the services of the great leader of an old generation. But his last years were basically happy ones. The old political feuds disappeared. New Englanders, such as George Ticknor and Daniel Webster, vied with Virginians in making pilgrimages to Monticello. Most gratifying of all was the reconciliation with his old rival, John Adams, and the eager exchange of ideas that followed. Together the two old men watched Madison, Monroe, and John Quincy Adams carry on a republican tradition to which both subscribed. Together they passed from this life on July 4, 1826, the fiftieth anniversary of American independence.

The fruition of many hopes that had been in doubt at the time of Jefferson's departure from office—demise of the old Federalist party, downfall of Napoleon, moral victory over Britain, and acquisition of new territory in the Floridas—signified a major change in his relations with France. When the European wars ended and Napoleon was sent into distant exile, the former President abandoned France as America's bulwark against the hostility of Britain, partly because the defeated nation lacked its old power, partly because the new Bourbon regime was too closely associated with the anti-republican reaction which was sweeping most of Europe, but mostly because he had lost much of his fear of Britain. Enervated by the exhaustions of war, England had as much to dread from the new combinations of European powers as had the United States. Indeed, Jefferson believed that Britain had more to fear from the constant turmoil on the Continent, since the United States had grown strong enough to turn its back upon Europe without worry about reprisal. After 1815 it had no need for a protector such as Louis XVI or fraternal allies such as the early revolutionaries had aspired to be.

For France as a nation and for Frenchmen as individuals he felt the same affection he had always known, a feeling he could never have for Great Britain. In his declining years, he enjoyed giving avuncular advice to a country which with care could some day win many of the privileges enjoyed by Americans. He had forgotten how the spectacle of the French Revolution had once hypnotized him, and remembered only that the misfortunes which befell that country occurred because she had not followed the plan of reform he had outlined in 1789. Having never understood the extent to which the governments of the Revolutions and their successors had betrayed his faith, or recognized his miscalculations about the Revolution itself, he did not find it difficult to be optimistic about the future of France.

Jefferson's departure from Washington in 1809 for his home at Monticello brought no change in his views concerning the international scene. As long as Napoleon remained in power and at war with the British navy, he continued to aver that the "Leviathan of the Sea" was the chief threat to America's security. In the solitude of the Virginia piedmont he dwelt upon prejudices against Britain and hopes for a French victory. Instead of acting as a moderating influence upon President Madison, Jefferson helped to stimulate his old friend's wrath against Britain.[1] The weaknesses in Madison's leadership that resulted in a declaration of war received no check from his former chief. In fact, the War of 1812 appeared to Jefferson to be the logical extension of the embargo program, and the results he had expected from the embargo were just those he hoped war would bring in 1812.

Reflecting carefully on the plight of his country, Jefferson weighed the virtues and faults of each belligerent and found the British to be more dangerous than ever before. Beyond the fact that Napoleon, without a navy, could not easily disturb the United States, he particularly noted that the French Empire lacked the stability and permanency of Britain. The Emperor's personality was as distasteful to him as ever, and his regime was admittedly the most violent and the most ruthless in Europe. But it was also the most ephemeral. When the dictator died, the flimsy structure he had erected would collapse with him. British power, on the other hand, was all the more intimidating because it could survive the death of its chief of state.[2] The implications of this unpleasant reflection were so inimical to

---

1. Federalists and their sympathizers made no secret of their belief that TJ controlled Madison's decisions. While TJ offered his advice on many issues, there was no conscious effort on his part to dictate policy and no uniform practice of acceptance on Madison's part. See Roy J. Honeywell, "President Jefferson and His Successor," *American Historical Review, 156* (October, 1940), 64–75. During the War of 1812 TJ reduced his correspondence with Madison to avoid charges of meddling. He was human enough, however, to resent the times when he did offer advice and Madison refused it. TJ to Monroe, May 30, 1813, L&B, *13*, 250–52; TJ to Madison, June 18, 1813, ibid., *13*, 259–60.

2. TJ to Caesar Rodney, February 10, 1810, ibid., *12*, 357–58; TJ to Robert Patterson, September 11, 1811, ibid., *13*, 87.

American interests in 1810 and 1811 that Jefferson appeared more disposed to accept a complete French victory over Britain than he had had been in the time of the embargo; "a *republican Emperor*" would at least reserve the United States for the last step in his march to world domination.[3] While Jefferson may have felt no more liking for the Emperor as an individual or any more trust in his promises than before, he was not awed by France. Britain, on the other hand, both frightened and angered him.

His disquisitions on the sins of foreign nations, and on the mortal sins of Britain in particular, were not made on the sole basis of past experience. He considered them in the light of new actions which the warring powers took against neutral America. Britain once again was the chief offender. The British foreign minister, George Canning, repudiated in 1809 a newly made agreement with the United States whereby each country would repeal punitive laws directed against the other. Canning's recall of Erskine from the post of British minister to the United States was technically justified because Erskine had not followed his instructions; but his tactless way of handling the matter added fuel to the fire of Anglophobia in America. Jefferson was all the more upset by this new evidence of British perfidy, because he had hoped that a real truce with Britain would permit the United States to deal more resolutely with Napoleon.[4]

Seeking revenge for this blow, the United States fell into the next snare of the wily French Emperor by scrapping the non-intercourse system, which had replaced the embargo, in favor of Macon's Bill Number 2 of 1810. Knowing that restoration of American trade with the belligerents would serve the British cause, Napoleon induced Madison to accept a purposely ambiguous announcement of the revocation of the Berlin and Milan decrees as meeting all the requirements of the Macon

3. TJ to Madison, April 19 and 27, 1809, ibid., *12*, 274, 276–77; TJ to John Langdon, March 5, 1810, ibid., *12*, 375. TJ's italics.

4. TJ to W. C. Nicholas, May 25, 1809, Ford, *11*, 107–08; TJ to Madison, June 16, 1809, ibid., *11*, 112.

Bill. Jefferson was no less willing to accept these French professions, even if they were not made in good faith.[5]

To trust Napoleon's statements in the fact of new hostile actions against American ships and sailors and in the absence of any official document canceling the Berlin and Milan decrees required the President to shut his eyes to reality. Actually, Madison placed no more faith in Napoleon's pledges than did Jefferson; he frankly expressed his skepticism about France's promises and pondered dolefully over the advisability of declaring war on both countries.[6] He shut his eyes to reality not by trusting the French but by allowing the crimes of the British and the desire for American expansion to push Napoleon's rapacity into the background.[7]

The corrosive issues of neutral rights and impressment were not the only ones that brought the United States into war with Britain. America's desire for continental expansion inflamed passions in the West and South, and not the least articulate voice among the expansionists was Jefferson's, urging his countrymen to observe that America had more to gain from a war with Britain than from a war with France. He applauded Madison's decision to send occupation troops into Spanish Florida to protect American interests and advised him to take over East Florida as well as West Florida lest Britain, as Spain's ally, seize it first on the pretext of helping the Spanish against Napoleon.[8]

Florida was small pickings compared with the vast territory to the north which Britain could cede to the United States. Control of Canada would give new riches and power to the young republic and bring security to the pioneers whose lives

5. TJ to Mazzei, December 29, 1813, Jefferson Papers (L.C.), 200.

6. Madison to TJ, March 18, 1811, and May 25, 1812, *The Writings of James Madison, 8,* 134–35 and 190–91.

7. C. C. Tansill, "Robert Smith," in Bemis, *American Secretaries of State, 3,* 177. See also Irving Brant, *James Madison: President, 1809–1812* (Indianapolis, 1956), pp. 481–83. Brant places most of the blame, however, on Federalist and British leadership.

8. TJ to John Wayles Eppes, January 5, 1811, Ford, *11,* 160–61. See Julius W. Pratt, *Expansionists of 1812* (New York, 1925), pp. 69–75.

were constantly being menaced by British-led Indians. "The possession of that country," Jefferson wrote, "secures our women and children forever from the tomahawk and scalping knife, by removing those who excite them."[9] The acquisition of Canada had long been in his mind, although obscured by other problems that had diverted his energies when he was President. His only objection to Madison's declaration of war was its timing; war should have been declared when the weather first permitted entrance of American troops into Canada.[10]

Jefferson made no move to halt the course of the conflict; rather he anticipated it and welcomed it. He did not prefer war to diplomacy; in his view, diplomacy had failed with the downfall of the embargo, and the only method of handling the British thenceforth was war. Having stoically accepted the ultimate necessity of war, he could afford to brush aside the malice and greed of Napoleon as minor problems.[11] Jefferson's pacifism, which had been a dominant factor in his policies as a statesman, had always had a limit. When it was reached, he sought America's advantage from her own war just as in the past he had sought advantage from wars of other powers.

The calmness with which the former President accepted news of war with Britain was increased by his complacent expectation that American soldiers would have little difficulty in occupying Canada. Britain did not have many men in Canada; she was too absorbed in her European ventures to man her American possessions adequately. "The acquisition of Canada this year, as far as the neighborhood of Quebec, will be a mere matter of marching, and will give us experience for the attack of Halifax the next, and the final expulsion of England from the American continent."[12] To be sure, Jefferson anticipated some hardships, such as the burning of New York and other seaport towns, but

9. TJ to John Adams, June 11, 1812, L&B, *13*, 161.

10. TJ to Madison, June 29, 1812, ibid., *13*, 172; TJ to Madison, March 26, 1812, Jefferson Papers (L.C.), *195*.

11. TJ to Madison, August 17, 1809, L&B, *12*, 305–06; TJ to Walter Jones, March 5, 1810, ibid., *12*, 372–73.

12. TJ to Duane, August 4, 1812, ibid., *13*, 180–81.

he had hopes that incendiaries, recruited by the "starving manufacturers" of Britain who would be deprived of gainful employment by the lack of markets, would amply compensate for such a catastrophe with retaliatory attacks upon London!"[13] As for probable British victories on the high seas, American privateers would counterbalance their damage with destruction of Britain's merchant marine. So confident was the squire of Monticello of America's ability to defeat Britain that he was not sorry that Congress had learned too late about the revocation of the orders in council which should have removed the immediate cause of hostilities. If the British wanted peace now, they should surrender Canada as indemnification for ships and men seized during the past twenty years and as security against further attacks by them or by their Indian allies.[14] "The British government seem to be doing late, what done earlier might have prevented war; to wit: repealing the orders in Council. But it should take more to make peace than to prevent war. The sword once drawn, full justice must be done."[15]

For the United States to win its objectives—new territory in America, destruction of British commerce, and the humbling of British sea power—complete cooperation with the French Empire should have been the logical result of her entry into the war. The United States and France were fighting a common enemy, and Jefferson counted heavily upon Napoleon's support for success. Only by being assured that British forces would be tied down in Europe could Americans expect free rein in America; only the Continental System could shake the financial structure of Britain. The former President showed his understanding of America's dependence on France by approving Napoleon's invasion of Russia, which coincided with America's

13. TJ to General Thaddeus Kosciusko, June 28, 1812, ibid., *13*, 169. TJ had long believed that England's industrial system would fall apart once its American sources of supply were cut off. As late as the summer of 1814 he still had visions of starving workers eager to help America by punishing their ruling classes for the loss of their livelihoods. See TJ to Thomas Cooper, September 10, 1814, ibid., *14*, 186.

14. TJ to Thomas Letre, August 8, 1812, ibid., *13*, 185–86.

15. TJ to Robert Wright, August 8, 1812, ibid., *13*, 184.

initial war moves. "The exclusion of their [British] commerce from the United States, and the closing of the Baltic against it, which the present campaign in Europe will effect, will accomplish the catastrophe already so far advanced on them."[16]

The United States government nevertheless maintained the fiction of fighting its own separate war and saw no occasion of making this an excuse to fraternize with the Emperor. Jefferson heartily concurred in this attitude. It was, first of all, good politics to disassociate America's action from France's war against Europe. Claims for spoliations and amends for imprisonment of American seamen remained a sore point in Franco-American relations.[17] Any talk of open alliance with the French would have invoked the wrath not only of the Federalists and the Francophobes, but also of those Republicans who detested the Napoleonic dictatorship. There was no need for a change of status between the two countries; France, it was felt, would perform the service of tying up the British in Europe, no matter what course the United States would pursue.[18]

Jefferson's attitude toward the two major adversaries during the War of 1812 was probably more confused than subtle. Clinging to his old theme that Britain was America's principal enemy, he seemed early in the war to look favorably upon a thorough defeat of the British. The next step was to be war with France if necessary.[19] Single-handedly, it seemed, the American David could take on the two Goliaths of Europe and defeat them each in turn!

As the war progressed and the invasion of Canada proved more troublesome, Jefferson reflected further upon this scheme and found it wanting. It finally occurred to him that despite all the obstacles Providence might throw in the way of Napoleon's conquest of the United States, a victorious Emperor

16. TJ to William Duane, August 4, 1812, ibid., *13*, 181.
17. Monroe's report to the President, July 12, 1813, ASP FR, *3*, 609–12.
18. See L. S. Kaplan, "France and Madison's Decision for War, 1812," *Mississippi Valley Historical Review, 50* (1964), 652–71.
19. TJ to Robert Wright, August 8, 1812, L&B, *13*, 184–85.

might easily possess the British fleet and all the resources of the British Empire, combining therewith the power of the "Leviathan of the Sea" with that of the "Mammoth of the Land." "The success of Bonaparte in the battle of Dresden," he observed, "and repair of the checks given by Bernadotte and Blucher, which I have no doubt he will soon effect, added to the loss of Canada, will produce a melancholy meeting between the Executive of England and its parliament. And should it overset the ministry it might give us peace with England, and consequently war with all those arrayed against her in Europe, which will hardly mend our situation."[20]

Therefore, the United States would do better to let the two powers battle themselves to mutual exhaustion so that neither would have strength left to hurt smaller countries. He decided that it was wise for the United States to send grain to British troops in Spain where they were locked in combat with the French, because if the British should be starved out of Spain, he feared they would be sent to the American theater of operations. On the other hand, the United States should do nothing to interfere with the French campaign in the Baltic, for there France was serving our cause by shutting off Britain's manufactures from that sea and hence from the Continent, thereby "assisting us in her reduction to extremity."[21] So difficult was the choice that "we know not what to fear, and, only standing to our helm, must abide, with folded arms, the issue of the storm."[22]

While the devious course of Jefferson's opinions on foreign policy pointed toward a stalemate in Europe as the desirable result for America, the logic of his country's position in Europe's war indicated service to French interests. Understandably, his

20. TJ to T. M. Randolph, November 14, 1813, Jefferson Papers (L.C.), 200.

21. TJ to James Ronaldson, January 12, 1813, L&B, *13*, 205–06. A year later TJ changed his mind about a French invasion of Russia when he realized that a Napoleonic victory would "lay at his feet the whole continent of Europe." TJ to Thomas Leiper, January 1, 1814, ibid., *14*, 43–44.

22. TJ to Mrs Trist, June 10, 1814, Jefferson Papers (Massachusetts Historical Society).

followers were never so mystified about his views as they were at this time. If a French conquest of Europe was inimical to the United States, why make common cause in war? How was he to explain a policy that advocated a French victory, but not too much of a French victory? And Jefferson was forced to make explanations, for even in retirement he was considered the fountainhead of all wisdom in the Republican party and as such was expected to exert considerable influence upon the Madison administration.[23] The issue of friendship with France divided Republicans into two groups: those whose contempt for Bonaparte as a destroyer of liberty made them as anxious for his defeat as for Britain's, and those whose hatred for Britain transformed Bonaparte into an agent of republicanism. Since Jefferson's ideas on America's relations with France were susceptible to both interpretations, it was not surprising that both groups claimed him for their patron.

The consequence of a misunderstanding arising from the intraparty confusion of war aims could have been political embarrassment to the country's war effort as well as personal grief for Jefferson. For the most part he was successful in reconciling the two factions without bringing the issues into the public eye, but in one instance he was forced to admit to hostility toward both major belligerents so openly that he feared the French minister would lodge a protest claiming his statements were lending comfort to the enemy.[24] The cause of this storm was the controversial figure, George Logan, an ardent supporter of the French Revolution until the rise of Bonaparte. He was the idealistic and perhaps naïve Pennsylvania Quaker who had made a visit to Europe in the summer of 1798 to find out for himself whether the French government

23. The Republican journalist, William Duane, had even assumed that the old master would replace James Monroe as Secretary of State after the fiasco in Canada. TJ was gratified by this show of loyalty and deemed it honorable "for the general of yesterday to act as a corporal today, if his service can be useful to his country." But he claimed that he was too old to be of service. William Duane to TJ, September 20, 1812, Jefferson Papers (L.C.), *196;* TJ to Duane, October 1, 1812, L&B, *13,* 186–87.

24. TJ to Thomas Leiper, January 4, 1814, Jefferson Papers (L.C.), *200.*

intended to make war upon the United States. Although the
Federalists had reprimanded him by passage of the Logan Act
penalizing private citizens undertaking such missions to foreign
governments, Logan's report of the friendliness of the Directory
influenced many Americans, including Thomas Jefferson. Fifteen years later, Logan's missionary zeal was no less strong,
except that his love for France had been converted into hatred
for the dictator. Making another trip to Europe, this time to
England, he found in 1810 confirmation for his prejudices, just
as he had in 1798. England was free and powerful and much
less under the control of the sordid commercial class than most
Americans imagined.[25] Hence, when the Anglo-American war
broke out, Logan considered it his duty to inform Jefferson
that an honorable treaty could be made with the British if the
former President asserted his influence on Madison.[26]

Jefferson had standard answers for Republican critics who
opposed America's fighting France's enemy. He would usually
marshal his old arguments admitting the villainies of Napoleon
and France's animosity toward the United States, while at the
same time claiming that British enmity was more immediate
and more threatening to the national security. Possibly in defer-
ence to Logan's emotional state, his reply in this instance
emphasized more forcefully than was customary his own horror
of the imperial regime: "No man on earth has stronger detesta-
tion than myself of the unprincipled tyrant who is deluging
the continent of Europe with blood." The letter also contained
the usual qualifying remarks about his hope of "seeing England
forced to just terms of peace with us," a hope that could be
realized only through the agency of Napoleon.[27] Whether
Logan misunderstood the qualification or purposely misconstrued the letter is not clear. What is clear was his release to
the press of an excerpt that presented the former President as
an enemy of France and an apparent opponent of the war.[28]

25. Logan to TJ, September 18 and December 9, 1813, ibid.
26. Logan to TJ, September 18, 1813, ibid.
27. TJ to Logan, October 3, 1813, L&B, *13*, 384–87.
28. It appeared in *Poulson's American Advertiser*, Philadelphia, December 6, 1813.

Publication of Jefferson's condemnation of Napoleon immediately antagonized Republicans, like Thomas Leiper of Philadelphia, who considered the French to be performing a noble service, if unwittingly, in fighting Britain and forces of monarchical reaction. Leiper wrote Jefferson a letter of rebuke, lecturing him on the consequences of a British victory. The triumphant British, he foresaw, "would not suffer a Cockboat of any other nation to swim the Ocean." The only consolation he could find in the old statesman's apparent Anglophilism was the possibility that the letter was a forgery.[29] Jefferson did not fail him. Shocked "by the infidelity of one with whom I was formerly intimate, but who has abandoned the American principles out of which that intimacy grew, and become the bigoted partisan of England," he explained the details of Logan's "infidelity" to Leiper.[30] Despite the unpleasantness that this contretemps caused him,[31] the incident made it perfectly clear that when he was forced to choose between Britain and France, his choice fell to the latter.

The fact that the Treaty of Ghent in December, 1814 ended the War of 1812 without entailing the loss of any American territory testified to the essential truth of one of Jefferson's favorite theses: Europe's troubles were America's opportunity. With Napoleon brought to heel and banished to the island of Elba, Britain was master of Europe as well as of the high seas and hence was in a position to impose her will upon the hapless United States whose campaigns against British America had

---

29. Leiper to TJ, December 9, 1813, Jefferson Papers (L.C.), *200*.
30. TJ to Leiper, January 1, 1814, L&B, *14*, 41–45.
31. It is worth noting that TJ's cry of betrayal did not signify the severance of his relations with Logan. TJ never wanted to lose a friend; he went out of his way to renew ties with Logan as he had done with others—Paine, Monroe, William Short—who had abused his friendship on various occasions. It is possible that Logan had not realized what he had done. He actually wrote TJ, thanking him for what he obviously considered to be support of his views. Logan to TJ, December 9, 1813, Jefferson Papers (L.C.), *200*. Not until after the war did TJ express to Logan his resentment over the incident, and then he couched it in gentle terms. TJ to Logan, May 19, 1816, Ford, *11*, 525–26.

failed even while the French Emperor was still ruler of the Continent. If Britain did not complete her reconquest of America, a prominent deterrent was the difficulties facing her in the redivision of Europe. Worn out by long years of warfare, Britain envisaged sufficient obstacles at the Vienna peace tables —potential squabbles among the victorious allies and the possible return of Napoleon—to dampen her ardor for revenge upon the Americans.

The retired statesman of Monticello saw none of this at first. When the Emperor departed for Elba in the spring of 1814, Jefferson expected that his country would be exposed to the unchecked wrath of the British, to their lust for reconquest.[32] Contemplation of this frightening prospect, in which the burning of Washington seemed to have been only a prelude, made him regard Napoleon in an almost favorable light. He remembered that "he gave employment to much of the force of the nation who was our common enemy" and that "diabolical as they paint the enemy, he burnt neither public edifices nor private dwellings. It was reserved for England to show that Bonaparte, in atrocity, was an infant to their ministers and their generals."[33]

While Jefferson mourned the loss of French power and expressed his fear of the anger of Britain, he observed Britain's disposition to talk peace and urged Americans to meet her efforts at least halfway. The invasion of Canada having ended in ignominious failure, Jefferson made little mention of territorial ambitions as being obstacles in the way of American reconciliation with Britain. As for the issues of neutral rights and impressment, he hoped that the conclusion of the European war would make them academic. He personally was happy to do his part in calming British passions by letting it be known that he had never really been hostile to the British people; he merely disliked some of the principles, such as their interpreta-

32. TJ to John Melish, December 10, 1814, L&B, *14*, 219.
33. TJ to Thomas Cooper, September 10, 1814, ibid., *14*, 186; TJ to William Crawford, February 11, 1815, ibid., *14*, 240. TJ to Monroe, January 1, 1815, ibid., *14*, 226–27.

tion of neutral rights, and even those principles would be acceptable if the United States might thereby escape from the war.[34] He approved of the work of the peace negotiators, although the posthumous victory of American arms at New Orleans gave him back some of his old boldness: "I presume that, having spared to the pride of England her formal acknowledgment of the atrocity of impressment in an article of the treaty, she will concur in a convention for relinquishing it."[35] The last was only face-saving bluster.

As soon as the United States was released from war with Britain, Jefferson's attitude toward France gradually became more hostile. Not that he admitted his mistake in having supported the imperial regime in the past. On the contrary, his disgust for the stupidity of the restored Bourbons made him welcome for a moment the return of Napoleon from Elba as a defender of "the cause of his nation, and that of all mankind, the rights of every people to independence and self-government."[36] But with the British threat removed, these thoughts were no more than an expression of anger at the greed of the Coalition and its Bourbon puppet; he knew that France could never enjoy lasting peace under a Bonaparte. No matter how democratic his guise, the result would be military despotism for France and renewal of conflict for the world. Jefferson did not regret Waterloo very long.[37]

Had he still been disturbed by the specter of a British war or of British attacks on neutral rights, he might have felt more solicitous about the fate of the exiled Emperor of the French. But the fear of Britain that had haunted him for forty years had vanished. The world was at peace, and the new French

34. TJ to Short, November 28, 1814, ibid., *14*, 212–13; TJ to John Adams, July 5, 1814, ibid., *14*, 146–47; TJ to Caesar Rodney, March 16, 1815, ibid., *14*, 285–86.

35. TJ to Madison, March 23, 1815, ibid., *14*, 291–92.

36. TJ to Correa de Serra, June 28, 1815, ibid., *14*, 330; TJ to Adams, August 10, 1815, *The Adams-Jefferson Letters*, *2*, 454; TJ to Mazzei, August 9, 1815, Ford, *11*, 483.

37. TJ to Du Pont, May 15, 1815, L&B, *14*, 297–98; TJ to Adams, June 10 and August [11], 1815, *The Adams-Jefferson Letters*, *2*, 441–42, 454.

government that succeeded Napoleon would have been a poor shield even if the United States had still been inclined to look to France for protection. Under the feeble but oppressive leadership of the Bourbons, France after 1815 was just one of a group of Continental powers that, according to Jefferson, dedicated themselves to the eradication of all the liberal ideals which America represented.

As the British menace receded into the past, Jefferson saw the island kingdom in an entirely different perspective. Despite an odious government and the persistence of supercilious anti-American sentiment, he was satisfied that the long and hard wars of the past twenty years had weakened Britain's economy to such a degree that she had lost her ability to hurt the United States. Excessive development of an economy based on finance and commerce had produced, in the opinion of the moral philosopher of Virginia, overexpansion of important industries, ruinous taxation, dangerous extremes in wealth, and the prospect of national bankruptcy in the near future. England's only sensible course would be to adopt a policy of "retrenchment" and "frugality" and to renounce her pretension to ruling the world. Since the men in power would not be willing to sacrifice their "flesh-pots" to the welfare of the majority, a revolution would be required to inaugurate that program. Then British habits of self-government would enable that nation to follow the path of the United States toward peace and prosperity! Even the sane voice of Adams gently mocking these predictions did not shake his faith in the conviction that Albion was falling from "her transcendent sphere" to a more modest but not an insignificant place among the nations of the world.[38]

The Virginia soothsayer was not dismayed by Adams' skepticism. Jefferson's predictions were unimportant in comparison with his new conception of the balance of power out of which they had arisen. It placed Britain as a third force, standing between republican United States and the militant reactionary

38. TJ to Monroe, October 16, 1816, L&B, *15*, 79–80; TJ to John Adams, November 25, 1816, *The Adams-Jefferson Letters, 2*, 496–97; Adams to TJ, December 16, 1816, ibid., *2*, 502.

monarchies of Europe which were anxious to undo every vestige of the French Revolution.

There is no better evidence of the role in the balance of power to which Jefferson now consigned Britain than the advice he gave to President Monroe in 1823 concerning the threat of the Holy Alliance to reconquer Latin America on behalf of weak Spain. He had no more personal affection for the British at this time than in earlier years, nor did he believe their government to be more friendly to American aspirations than before. He even suggested that Britain's opposition to the Holy Alliance was only a sham, at best a selfish pursual of her own private interests in Latin America.[39] Nevertheless, some of those private interests coincided with America's needs, and when the President asked him whether the United States should accept Britain's proposals for a joint guarantee of Latin America against the attacks of Europe, he urged Monroe to accept the offer, so that the British fleet might remove the possibility of hostile intervention by the Continental alliance.[40]

Jefferson considered cooperation with Britain on this issue to be perfectly consistent with his hope of keeping America out of the jealousies, complicated alliances, and foreign principles of Europe. He advocated closer ties with England only because "the war in which the present proposition might engage us, should that be its consequence, is not her war, but ours."[41] But the need for cooperation with Britain, or with any other

39. TJ to Monroe, June 11, 1823, L&B, *15*, 436–39.
40. Monroe to TJ, October 17, 1823, *The Writings of James Monroe, 6*, 342; TJ to Monroe, October 24, 1823, L&B, *15*, 477–80.
41. TJ to Monroe, October 24, 1823, ibid., *15*, 478. Despite Monroe's rejection of TJ's advice, T. R. Schellenberg, in his "Jeffersonian Origins of the Monroe Doctrine," *Hispanic American Historical Review, 14* (1934), 1–31, claims that too much credit has been given to J. Q. Adams for formulating the Doctrine. The principle of nonintervention mutually applied by Europe and the United States was peculiarly Jeffersonian. He further claims it as an example of French influence upon TJ, since the latter first found the idea expressed in the writings of Abbé de Pradt. A more probable explanation is that the doctrine of abstention from the affairs of Europe was widely shared by the leaders of the country and owed its origins as much to the experiences gained from the Franco-American alliance as to a

nation, for that matter, would not last much longer. America was maturing so fast that she no longer needed a patron to protect her from hostile powers. Britain's service was only temporary and of far less importance to the nation's security than had been France's aid a generation earlier. The time was coming, he exulted, when the United States would be strong enough to sever all ties with the rest of the world and announce itself militarily and economically self-sufficient. In twenty years "we shall be twenty millions in number, and forty in energy," and then "old Europe will have to lean on our shoulders, and to hobble along by our side, under the monkish trammels of priests and kings . . . as [best] she can."[42]

In his last years Jefferson gloried in the vision of a greater America of the future and in the knowledge that he could take much of the credit for the magnificent accomplishments of his country. Forgotten were his deviations from his own policies of continental expansion and of abstention from European quarrels; his miscalculations about the French Revolution; his unsuccessful attempts to outwit Napoleon. To the last, he never admitted, or even realized, that French imperialism before 1815 might have been a greater threat to America's sovereignty than British arrogance had been.

Unlike the controversial issue of his views on France's foreign policy, Jefferson's past errors in interpreting the French Revolution could not be wholly ignored. His reconciliation with John Adams had given the Sage of Quincy opportunities to even up in a friendly correspondence some old scores that were too good to be overlooked. Adams jibed frequently and effectively at the opinions which Jefferson had once held on the Revolution, particularly his assumption that it would lead the French people to a successful establishment of a free republican govern-

French priest writing in 1820. There is a discussion of the question in Bemis, *John Quincy Adams and the Foundations of American Foreign Policy*, pp. 364–66.

42. TJ to Du Pont, December 31, 1815, L&B, *14*, 371; TJ to John Adams, August 1, 1816, *The Adams-Jefferson Letters*, *2*, 484.

ment. Adams, on the other hand, had always been convinced that a nation of illiterates, untrained in the arts of self-government, could never succeed in such a scheme. Without mentioning Jefferson specifically, he mocked the theoreticians who foolishly believed that by some mystical process France would undergo a metamorphosis from which she would emerge a full-fledged republic. Because of his skepticism, he complained, he suffered unpopularity. But in the light of the events of the past twenty years, who was right? This was the question with which the old Federalist ended many of his letters to his former colleague.[43]

Adams' somewhat bitter reminders of bygone days left their mark on Jefferson, but not in the manner expected. Jefferson readily admitted the failure of the French Revolution but not his involvement with it. With some justice he separated himself from the category of "ideologist" in which Adams had placed the inexperienced French philosophers, and claimed that the sorrows of France were due in large part to her neglect to profit from his insistence upon moderation in reform. "France," he claimed, "after crushing and punishing the conspiracy of Pilnitz, went herself deeper and deeper into the crimes she had been chastising."[44] The whole nation, and not just Robespierre or Bonaparte, was responsible, therefore, for the misfortunes that followed. By agreeing with Adams' criticism of the French Revolution, Jefferson was able to dismiss the main point of his correspondent: that he had approved of and benefited politically from the very events that he was denouncing. He gave no indication that he had ever set aside, upon his return to the United States in 1789, the counsel of moderation which he had given to his French disciples, or that he had ever been jubilant over the excesses of the Revolution in 1792.

The ability of the philosopher–statesman to expunge the unpleasant memories from his mind helped to protect him from

43. Two notable letters of Adams to TJ (June 30 and July 13, 1813, *The Adams-Jefferson Letters*, 2, 346–48 and 354–56) struck hard at TJ's naïveté about the Revolution.
44. TJ to John Adams, January 11, 1816, ibid., 2, 459.

the cynicism of his Massachusetts friend. The unhappy fate of the French Revolution consequently did not spoil his enthusiasm either for revolution in general or for France in particular. With considerable verve he challenged Adams' thesis that democracy has no more inherent virtues than has autocracy or oligarchy. Democratic government, in Jefferson's eyes, was a social instrument especially adapted for a country like America where every man could own property and feel a stake in the support of society. The people of the United States, trained by their environment and traditions, "may safely and advantageously reserve to themselves a wholsome controul over their public affairs."[45] Nor were foreign nations to be excluded from these privileges when they had proved themselves sufficiently prepared to assume the responsibilities of democracy. It did not matter that the French Revolution itself had failed, for even in failing it had publicized the blessings of self-government, and had thereby prevented the peoples of Europe from being satisfied with the return of the old autocrats. Progress was inevitable.[46] Thus Jefferson could accept without question the assurances of Gallatin and Lafayette that the seeds of liberty implanted in France by the Revolution were sprouting amidst the hostility of the restored Bourbons.[47]

In his last days, Jefferson was again the schoolmaster showing his devoted pupils how they might acquire the knowledge of the teacher. Lafayette, Du Pont, von Humboldt, and Tracy were all encouraged to prepare themselves for the liberal government of the future. As long as they did not try to proceed too quickly,

45. TJ to Adams, October 28, 1813, ibid., 2, 391—his most vigorous reply to Adams' attacks.

46. TJ to Baron Quesnai de Rochemont, May 18, 1818, Jefferson Papers (University of Virginia).

47. Gallatin, Minister to France in 1815, reported the flourishing of a revolutionary legacy that the Restoration was unable to destroy: the people's independence of priest and noble. Gallatin to TJ, September 6 and November 27, 1815, Jefferson Papers (L.C.), 204 and 205. Lafayette also gave reports which characteristically were much more optimistic than Gallatin's. Lafayette to TJ, December 10, 1817 and July 20, 1820, Chinard, ed., The Letters of Lafayette and Jefferson, pp. 391–98.

Europeans would eventually free themselves from their autocrats. The Revolution had given them a taste for freedom that they had lacked before; and, more important, it had given them some experience in self-government. The old man writing to his foreign friends in 1820 did not differ too much in his views on revolution from the diplomatist of 1789. France was still his favorite foreign nation, and despite all the sins of her rulers and citizens, he still expected her to lead Europe along the path of liberty.[48]

The Sage of Monticello was justified in identifying himself with the success of the American experiment. He had done more than his share to make the nation prosperous. He had helped to steer his country through the difficult days of infancy, and at the same time had held aloft the ideals of republicanism and democracy for the entire world to admire and adopt.

Throughout his public life France as a nation, as a people, and as a symbol exercised an influence upon his thoughts and actions that profoundly affected the nature of his services to the United States. Dramatically entering his life as a savior of the struggling colonies, she remained through most of his career the defender of his country against the potential enmity of the rest of the world. This initial attraction was further buttressed by the pleasure he found in partaking of French cultural life and in receiving the homage of the French intelligentsia.

Against this background have been placed the charges that he had been a loyal servant of France's foreign policy and a willing disciple of French revolutionary ideas. These charges, which have come down through the nineteenth and twentieth centuries, carry great weight, particularly since Jefferson did fall victim to the designs of French imperialism and to the magnetism of the Revolution.

But neither role was a conscious one. It is obvious that Jefferson always regarded himself, and with reason, as a teacher rather than a follower of the *idéologues*. It is equally obvious

48. TJ to Albert Gallatin, October 16, 1815, L&B, *14*, 359.

that Jefferson understood the importance to American security of an equilibrium in Europe. As he had asserted many times, the objective of the United States in any European struggle should be ultimate stalemate, leaving the belligerents too weak to significantly affect the sovereignty of small neutrals. Nevertheless, his confidence in America's powers of coercion and his preoccupation with the British menace led him to adopt a foreign policy that misread the scales of power. The freedom of action which he enjoyed in dealing with embattled Europe stemmed from an assumption that the balance was fundamentally in favor of the British. Thus he could risk supporting France's ambitions, secure in the knowledge that the services he was rendering would not affect the desired stalemate. While he recognized the evils of the dictator's regime, he saw an imbalance in the comparative positions of France and Britain which allowed diplomatic maneuvers that would not have been ventured had he been dealing with two countries equally dangerous to the United States.

He was not without his doubts about his balance-of-power policy. Periodically, he expressed fear concerning the consequences of a victory for either belligerent, but even in his darkest mood Jefferson would still take his chances with a victorious France, if such a choice had to be made. Those rare occasions when he spoke out in favor of an alliance with Britain or on the benignity of British sea power were prior to the intensification of the European wars and reflected either a devious gambit designed to extract concessions from the French or an errant faith in the friendliness of an occasional British ministry.

Jefferson's activities on behalf of France are difficult to explain on the basis of national interest. Granting the material and psychological damage done by British maritime practices and granting also the threat to America's sovereignty inherent in their actions, one may still claim that Britain's war was essentially a defense against the continuous pressure of Revolutionary and, later, Napoleonic imperialism, and the policies which disturbed or injured Americans were essentially by-products of Britain's response to that pressure.

Even if the United States had been buttressing the weaker power, the idea of competing so vigorously in the international arena was exceedingly dangerous when all adversaries were so much more powerful than herself. But Jefferson's policies, centering as they did on retaliation against Britain's past and future as well as present actions, and on using France to win Louisiana, pushed the country inexorably into the European maelstrom. Only by keeping out of Europe's wars could the plan of playing one country against the other be executed with any real success; by engaging ultimately in the war as a cobelligerent if not as a formal ally, the country deprived itself of the advantages Jefferson had anticipated. Once involved, the danger of being either overwhelmed by the superior force of the enemy or treated as a satellite by the powerful ally was far greater than the opportunity for making gains at the expense of both.

While the French Revolution was unquestionably a factor in shaping Jefferson's attitudes toward France, his foreign policy cannot be fairly attributed to its influence. France's potential service as America's agent in Europe was the critical factor in his view of the Revolution and of Napoleon. His successes as a statesman were always characterized by recognition of the importance of the European balance of power to America's survival, of the need for freedom from foreign entanglements in assuring independence, and of the value of a cautious diplomacy in advancing western expansion. In surmounting difficulties created in good measure by departures from these precepts, Jefferson helped to confirm the faith of the Founding Fathers in the special destiny that sets America apart from the Old World.

Bibliographical Note

This bibliography contains for the most part those materials from the
mass of Jeffersoniana that bear directly upon my treatment of the
relations between Jefferson and France.

General Works

Henry Adams, *History of the United States During the Administrations of Jefferson and Madison* (9 vols. New York, 1889–91).
    Although errors have been noted, lacunae filled in, and biases
attacked in the past three-quarters of a century, Adams' work
remains the classic against which all studies of Jefferson's presidency are measured.

Vernon L. Parrington, *Main Currents in American Thought: An
Interpretation of American Literature from the Beginnings to
1920* (3 vols. New York, 1927).
    Best expression of the view that Jefferson's idealism was the prod-
uct of French humanitarian doctrines.

Howard M. Jones, *America and French Culture, 1750–1848* (Chapel
Hill, 1927).
    An able study which expresses its disturbance over the frequent
failure of Jefferson's political behavior to reflect his Francophile
cultural sympathies.

Bernard Faÿ, *The Revolutionary Spirit in France and America: A
Study of Moral and Intellectual Relations between France and the
United States at the End of the Eighteenth Century,* trans. R.
Guthrie (New York, 1927).
    In his zeal to emphasize the affinity between the two countries Faÿ
makes excessive use of his imagination to replace gaps in facts.

Samuel Flagg Bemis, ed., *The American Secretaries of State and
Their Diplomacy* (10 vols. New York, 1927–29).
    Useful sketches of the individual secretaries by authorities in dip-

lomatic history. Of particular interest is the editor's own sketch of Jefferson.

Basil Willey, *The Eighteenth Century Background* (London, 1940). A literary survey of the ideas of the Enlightenment, with an interesting contrast between French and English contributions.

Arthur B. Darling, *Our Rising Empire* (New Haven, 1940). Comprehensive treatment of America's territorial expansion from the Revolution to the Louisiana Purchase, with emphasis on America's shifting relations with France. The book is marred by a difficult style.

A. Whitney Griswold, *Farming and Democracy* (New York, 1948). A chapter on Jefferson and the physiocrats suggests that the similarities in their philosophies are only superficial.

Durand Echeverria, *Mirage in the West: A History of the French Image of American Society to 1815* (Princeton, 1957). A sophisticated analysis of the philosophes' misconceptions about America. Jefferson is the major figure around whom the image is built.

John C. Miller, *The Federalist Era, 1789–1801* (New York, 1960). The best recent treatment of the period in which Hamilton is sympathetically treated.

Felix Gilbert, *To the Farewell Address: Ideas of Early American Foreign Policy* (Princeton, 1961). Provocative essays centering on the influences of the Enlightenment on the formulation of American foreign policy in the late colonial and early national periods.

Paul Varg, *Foreign Policies of the Founding Fathers* (East Lansing, 1964). A well-written synthesis of the contributions of contemporary scholarship to the interpretation of American foreign policy from the Revolution to the War of 1812.

Robert R. Palmer, *Age of the Democratic Revolution: A Political History of Europe and America, 1760–1800*. Vol. I—*The Challenge* (Princeton, 1959). Vol. II—*The Struggle* (Princeton, 1964). An impressive presentation of the inseparability of ideas and events in Europe and America of the eighteenth century.

Special Works

Monographs and articles on the Jeffersonian era

Charles D. Hazen, "Contemporary American Opinion of the French Revolution," *Johns Hopkins University Studies in Historical and Political Science, 16* (Baltimore, 1897).

France viewed through the eyes of prominent Americans, including Jefferson.

B. W. Bond, "The Monroe Mission to France, 1794–1796," *Johns Hopkins University Studies in Historical and Political Science, 25* (Baltimore, 1907).
Sympathetic to Monroe's position, although the author exposes his indiscretions as minister to France.

F. J. Turner, "The Origin of Genet's Projected Attack on Louisiana and the Floridas," *American Historical Review, 13* (1908), 650–71.
Turner notes Jefferson's participation in France's American projects.

Alfred Schalck de la Faverie, *Napoléon et l'Amérique: histoire des relations franco-américaines specialement envisagée au point de vue de l'influence Napoléonne, 1688–1815* (Paris, 1917).
One of the few works on the subject in French. It is a slipshod unsatisfactory survey of Franco-American relations.

Frank E. Melvin, *Napoleon's Navigation System: A Study of Trade Control During the Continental Blockade* (New York, 1919).
An authoritative study of the system based on materials from French, British, and American archives.

Frederick L. Nussbaum, *Commercial Policy in the French Revolution: A Study of the Career of G. J. A. Ducher* (Washington, D.C., 1923).
Emphasis on the strong influence of mercantilism on many of the leading revolutionists that led to opposition to commercial concessions to the United States.

———, "American Tobacco and French Politics, 1783–1789," *Political Science Quarterly, 40* (1925), 497–516.
An explanation of the difficulties Jefferson encountered as minister to France when he attempted to have the powers of the Farmers General reduced.

Samuel Flagg Bemis, *Jay's Treaty: A Study in Commerce and Diplomacy* (New York, 1923).
This monograph points out how Secretary of the Treasury Hamilton overshadowed Secretary of State Jefferson in shaping American policy toward the Franco-British war.

———, *Pinckney's Treaty: A Study of America's Advantage from Europe's Distress, 1783–1800* (Baltimore, 1926).
The subtitle gives the theme of Jefferson's overall conception of American foreign policy as well as his expectations from Spain.

———, "Washington's Farewell Address: A Foreign Policy of Independence," *American Historical Review, 39* (1934), 250–68.
The address was intended as a specific rebuke to France for interference in American domestic affairs.

156 BIBLIOGRAPHICAL NOTE

Mildred Stahl Fletcher, "Louisiana as a Factor in French Diplomacy from 1763 to 1800," *Mississippi Valley Historical Review, 17* (1930), 367–77.

Mrs. Fletcher's major point is that after 1796, during the period of tensions between France and the United States, the French worked consciously toward the repossession of Louisiana.

Charles M. Thomas, *American Neutrality in 1793: A Study in Cabinet Government* (New York, 1931).

Thomas concludes that American policy toward the belligerents was a cooperative effort of the Cabinet, with Washington as the balance between the two principals, Jefferson and Hamilton.

Arthur P. Whitaker, "The Retrocession of Louisiana in Spanish Policy," *American Historical Review, 39* (1934), 454–76.

Spain was not bullied into surrendering Louisiana to France. It was strictly a matter of bargaining.

E. Wilson Lyon, *Louisiana in French Policy, 1795–1804* (Norman, Okla., 1934).

The standard treatment of the development of French policy on Louisiana.

———, "The Franco-American Convention of 1800," *Journal of Modern History, 12* (1940), 305–34.

A perceptive but sketchy review of the negotiations.

Charles H. Van Duzer, "Contributions of the Ideologues to the French Revolution," *Johns Hopkins University Studies in Historical and Political Science, 53* (Baltimore, 1935).

Under the loose category of ideologues fall most of Jefferson's French friends, whom Van Duzer sees as the mainstay of the Directory and initial supporters of Bonaparte.

Irving Brant, "Edmund Randolph, Not Guilty!" *William and Mary Quarterly,* Third Series, 7 (1950), 179–98.

He blames Randolph's disgrace as Secretary of State in 1795 upon the mistranslation of the dispatches of French minister Fauchet.

Joseph I. Shulim, *The Old Dominion and Napoleon Bonaparte: A Study in American Opinion* (New York, 1952).

A relatively successful attempt to trace changing American views of Napoleon through careful analysis of Virginia newspapers.

Bradford Perkins, *The First Rapprochement: England and the United States, 1795–1805* (Philadelphia, 1955).

———, *Prologue to War: England and the United States, 1805–1812* (Berkeley and Los Angeles, 1961).

———, *Castlereagh and Adams: England and the United States, 1812–1823* (Berkeley and Los Angeles, 1964).

A three-part study that effectively exploits unpublished British manuscripts. While both parties bear responsibility for difficulties in Anglo-American relations, Perkins attributes the larger share of blame to shortcomings in American statecraft prior to the War of 1812.

Albert H. Bowman, "Jefferson, Hamilton, and American Foreign Policy," *Political Science Quarterly, 71* (1956).
Well-written presentation of Jefferson's positions on American foreign policy as Secretary of State.

Stephen Kurtz, *The Presidency of John Adams: The Collapse of Federalism, 1795–1800* (Philadelphia, 1957).
A vigorous defense of Adams' foreign policies, and particularly of the Convention of 1800.

Alexander DeConde, "Washington's Farewell Address, the French Alliance, and the Election of 1796," *Mississippi Valley Historical Review, 43* (1957), 641–58.
The emphasis is on the Address as a partisan Federalist doctrine.

———, *Entangling Alliance: Politics and Diplomacy under George Washington* (Durham, N.C., 1958).
A thorough examination of the Washington administration, judging it as the work of partisan pro-British Hamilton.

Arthur A. Richmond, "Napoleon and the Armed Neutrality of 1800: A Diplomatic Challenge to British Sea Power," *Royal Service Institution Journal, 104* (1959), 1–9.
An examination of the role that Bonaparte envisaged for the United States in the Armed Neutrality League of 1800.

Marshall Smelser, "The Federalist Period as an Age of Passion," *American Quarterly, 10* (1958), 391–419.
The author observes that violent emotions governed the politics of Federalists and Republicans alike. In the case of the former, the emotions proved to be suicidal.

Noble E. Cunningham, "Who Were the Quids?" *Mississippi Valley Historical Review, 50* (1963), 252–64.
Whatever they were, they were not John Randolph or his followers.

L. S. Kaplan, "France and Madison's Decision for War, 1812," *Mississippi Valley Historical Review, 50* (1964), 652–71.
The assertion that France's power was a factor in Madison's calculations about future victory over Britain is accompanied by recognition that Madison intended no alliance with France.

Julian P. Boyd, *Number 7: Alexander Hamilton's Secret Attempts To Control American Foreign Policy* (Princeton, 1964).
An indictment of Hamilton's relations with Britain during the Nootka Sound controversy.

Biographies of Jefferson's Contemporaries

Octavius Pickering and C. W. Upham, *The Life of Timothy Pickering* (4 vols. Boston, 1867–73).
A work of piety gathered from the manuscripts of Jefferson's most articulate and most violent Federalist opponent.

M. R. Conway, *The Life of Thomas Paine* (2 vols. New York and London, 1902).
Contains interesting extracts from Paine's writings, but otherwise is of little value.

Samuel E. Morison, *The Life and Letters of Harrison Gray Otis* (2 vols. New York and Boston, 1913).
This is as much a study of New England Federalism as it is a biography of Otis. It is especially useful for its Federalist approach to the embargo.

Eloise Ellery, *Brissot de Warville: A Study in the History of the French Revolution* (Boston and New York, 1915).
Brissot was an ardent admirer of America and of Jefferson during the latter's ministry to France.

Albert Beveridge, *The Life of John Marshall* (4 vols. Boston, 1916–19).
Unfriendly and often unfair to Jefferson.

Meade Minnegerode, *Jefferson, Friend of France, 1793: The Career of Edmond Charles Genet* (New York, 1928).
The title is an ironic misnomer. It is a bitter attack on Jefferson as the cause of Genet's downfall.

Irving Brant, *James Madison: Virginia Revolutionist* (Indianapolis, 1941).
———, *James Madison: Nationalist, 1780–1787* (Indianapolis, 1948).
———, *James Madison: Father of the Constitution, 1787–1800* (Indianapolis, 1950).
———, *James Madison: Secretary of State, 1800–1809* (Indianapolis, 1953).
———, *James Madison: President, 1809–1812* (Indianapolis, 1956).
———, *James Madison: Commander in Chief, 1812–1836* (Indianapolis, 1961).
Impressively documented if not always convincing support of Madison's accomplishments against the claims of friends and enemies alike.

E. Wilson Lyon, *The Man Who Sold Louisiana: The Career of François Barbé-Marbois* (Norman, Okla., 1942).
Biography of a sympathetic French statesman who handled American relations under both the Ancien Régime and Bonaparte.

Louis R. Gottschalk, *Lafayette and the Close of the American Revolution* (Chicago, 1942).

———, *Lafayette Between the American and French Revolutions* (Chicago, 1950).

Perceptive studies of the complex character of America's most useful friend in France in the years immediately preceding the French Revolution.

W. P. Cresson, *James Monroe* (Chapel Hill, 1946).

Surprisingly weak on Monroe's role in Jefferson's presidential administrations.

Raymond Walters, Jr., *Albert Gallatin: Jeffersonian Financier and Diplomat* (New York, 1957).

This well-balanced study supercedes Henry Adams' pioneer biography. Gallatin emerges as Jefferson's most judicious adviser.

John C. Miller, *Alexander Hamilton: Portrait in Paradox* (New York, 1959).

The best recent treatment of Jefferson's most distinguished opponent.

George Dangerfield, *Chancellor Robert R. Livingston of New York, 1746–1813* (New York, 1960).

A major work on a minor figure that illuminates the whole Jeffersonian era.

C. Page Smith, *John Adams* (2 vols. New York, 1962).

Exhaustive treatment of his subject, taking advantage of the availability of the Adams Papers in the Massachusetts Historical Society.

Jefferson

I. J. Cox, "Pan-American Policy of Jefferson and Wilkinson," *Mississippi Valley Historical Review, 1* (1914), 212–39.

Cox claims that Jefferson's ambitions in Florida influenced his views toward Napoleon during most of his presidency.

Albert J. Nock, *Jefferson* (New York, 1926).

An impressionistic approach and very perceptive. Unlike most biographies, it is built around Jefferson's visit to France.

W. K. Woolery, "The Relations of Thomas Jefferson to American Foreign Policy, 1783–1793," *Johns Hopkins University Studies in Historical and Political Science, 45* (Baltimore, 1927).

Useful monograph on Jefferson's service as a diplomatist and particularly helpful in explaining his French policies.

Louis M. Sears, *Jefferson and the Embargo* (Durham, N.C., 1927).

The standard treatise on the subject. The author sees the embargo originating in Jefferson's pacific disposition.

Gilbert Chinard, *Thomas Jefferson: The Apostle of Americanism* (Boston, 1929).
This is the best one-volume biography of Jefferson, with emphasis on his relations with France.

———, "Jefferson and the Physiocrats," *University of California Chronicle, 33* (1931), 18–31.
The economic ideas of Jefferson and the physiocrats, despite similarities, were derived from different assumptions about man and society.

T. R. Schellenberg, "Jeffersonian Origins of the Monroe Doctrine," *Hispanic American Historical Review, 45* (1934), 1–34.
In claiming that Jefferson has not received enough credit for his contributions to the doctrine of non-intervention, the author attributes Jefferson's ideas to de Pradt, a French priest and philosophe.

Roy J. Honeywell, "President Jefferson and His Successor," *American Historical Review, 46* (1940), 64–75.
No undue influence is seen exercised over Madison after Jefferson's retirement in 1809.

Adrienne Koch, *The Philosophy of Thomas Jefferson* (New York, 1943).
A penetrating study of Jefferson's thought. It is particularly useful as an alternative to Chinard's and Becker's interpretations.

———, *Jefferson and Madison: The Great Collaboration* (New York, 1950).
Well-written but superficial examination of the interlocking of the two careers, with Madison's occupying a position almost equal to that of Jefferson's.

Marie Kimball, *Jefferson: The Road to Glory, 1743–1776* (New York, 1943).

———, *Jefferson: War and Peace, 1776–1789* (New York, 1947).

———, *Jefferson: The Scene of Europe, 1786–1789* (New York, 1950).
Written with attention to illuminating details, but limited in value by poor style and confusing citations.

Philip M. Marsh, "Jefferson's Retirement as Secretary of State," *Pennsylvania Magazine of History, 69* (1945), 220–24.
A defense of Jefferson's motives for retiring from office.

———, "Jefferson's Conduct of the *National Gazette*," *Proceedings of New Jersey Historical Society, 63* (1945), 69–73.

Dumas Malone, *Jefferson and His Time*, Vol. 1: *Jefferson the Virginian* (Boston, 1948).

———, *Jefferson and His Time*, Vol. 2: *Jefferson and the Rights of Man* (Boston, 1951).

————, *Jefferson and His Time,* Vol. 3: *Jefferson and the Ordeal of Liberty* (Boston, 1962).
When it is completed, this project will be the most comprehensive of all Jefferson biographies.
Leonard D. White, *The Jeffersonians: A Study in Administrative History, 1801–1829* (New York, 1951).
Particularly useful for his views on the embargo.
Mary P. Adams, "Jefferson's Reactions to the Treaty of San Ildefonso," *Journal of Southern History, 21* (1955), 173–88.
An emphasis on Jefferson's militant response to the Spanish cession of Louisiana to France.
Robert R. Palmer, "The Dubious Democrat: Thomas Jefferson and Bourbon France," *Political Science Quarterly, 82* (1957), 488–504.
Evaluation of Jefferson's firsthand observations on the beginnings of the French Revolution from his vantage point as minister to France. The author emphasizes Jefferson's doubts of French abilities to attempt too drastic a revolution.
L. S. Kaplan, "Jefferson, the Napoleonic Wars, and the Balance of Power," *William and Mary Quarterly,* Third Series, *14* (1957), 196–217.
————, "Jefferson's Foreign Policy and Napoleon's Idéologues," *William and Mary Quarterly,* Third Series, *19* (1962), 344–59.
Merrill D. Peterson, *The Jefferson Image in the American Mind* (New York, 1960).
A major work of interpretation, with a valuable bibliographical essay appended.
————, "Thomas Jefferson and Commercial Policy 1783–1793," *William and Mary Quarterly,* Third Series, 22 (1965), 584–611.
A perceptive examination of Jefferson's attempt to use commerce as a weapon of foreign policy as minister to France and as secretary of state.

Printed Sources

Correspondence, Diaries, and Memoirs of Jefferson's Contemporaries

Etienne Clavière and Jacques Brissot de Warville, *New Travels in North America, in the Years 1780, 1781, and 1782* (2 vols. London, 1792).
This is an example of the idealism about America generated in France by her intelligentsia, in this case by two future Girondists.
François de la Rochefoucald-Liancourt, *Travels through the United States of America . . . in the Years 1795, 1796, and 1797* (2 vols. London, 1799).
An exiled liberal nobleman and an ardent admirer of Jefferson.

M. Lemontey, ed., *Mémoires de l'abbé Morellet* (2 vols. Paris, 1821).
One of the liberal clergy who used his influence in America's
behalf while Jefferson was minister to France.

M. Fournier Ainé, ed., *Mémoires, correspondance et manuscrits
du Général Lafayette* (16 vols. Paris, 1838).

George Gibbs, ed., *Memoirs of the Administrations of Washington
and John Adams* (2 vols. New York, 1846).
Selected from the papers of Oliver Wolcott, Federalist secretary
of the treasury under John Adams, the memoirs consist largely
of correspondence among Jefferson's enemies.

A. Ducasse, ed., *Correspondance de Napoléon Ier* (32 vols. Paris,
1869).
For all the importance Napoleon had for Jefferson's career, the
references to Jefferson or to America are few and slighting.

Henry Adams, ed., *The Writings of Albert Gallatin* (Philadelphia,
1879).

Henry P. Johnson, ed., *The Correspondence and Papers of John Jay*
(New York, 1890–93).
His principal links to Jefferson were in the years when Jefferson
was minister to France and Jay was secretary for foreign affairs.

Charles R. King, ed., *The Life and Correspondence of Rufus King*
(5 vols. New York, 1894–1900).
Federalist minister to England who continued in office under
Jefferson. Hostile to Jefferson but milder than most Federalist
critics.

S. M. Hamilton, ed., *The Writings of James Monroe* (7 vols. New
York, 1898–1903).

Gaillard Hunt, ed., *The Writings of James Madison* (9 vols. New
York, 1900–10).

Henry Cabot Lodge, ed., *The Works of Alexander Hamilton* (12
vols. New York, 1904).

Worthington C. Ford, ed., *Writings of John Quincy Adams* (7 vols.
New York, 1913–17).

Dunbar Rowland, ed., *The Letter Books of W. C. C. Claiborne,
1801–1816* (6 vols. Jackson, Miss., 1917).
First governor of Louisiana territory and strong advocate of
seizure of the Floridas.

Anne Cary Morris, ed., *A Diary of the French Revolution* (New
York, 1939).
Observations, rarely friendly, on Jefferson's activities in France
and as Secretary of State by Gouverneur Morris, Minister to
France, 1792–94.

John C. Fitzpatrick, ed., *The Writings of George Washington* (37
vols. Washington, D.C., 1931–41).

The most complete edition of Washington's works.

Howard R. Marraro, ed., *Memoirs of the Life and Peregrinations of the Florentine Philip Mazzei, 1730–1816* (New York, 1942).
One of Jefferson's oldest friends, and a neighbor after Mazzei's emigration to Virginia.

Louis R. Gottschalk, *Letters of Lafayette and Washington* (New York, 1944).
This collection contains many references to Jefferson, particularly in the early stages of their friendship.

François de Chastellux, *Travels in North America, in the Years 1780, 1781, and 1782,* ed. H. C. Rice, Jr. (2 vols. Chapel Hill, 1963).
The views of a liberal aristocrat and visitor to Monticello.

Writings of Jefferson

The Jefferson Papers, Collections of the Massachusetts Historical Society, Series 7, Vol. 1, 1900.
These concern private affairs for the most part and are selected from the Coolidge collection in Boston.

Paul L. Ford, ed., *The Works of Thomas Jefferson* (12 vols. New York, 1904).

———, *The Writings of Thomas Jefferson* (10 vols. New York, 1892–99).
Until the completion of the Princeton series the Ford editions are the most useful.

Andrew A. Lipscomb and Albert E. Bergh, eds., *The Writings of Thomas Jefferson* (20 vols. Washington, D.C., 1904).
The most voluminous completed edition, but editorial errors require the reader to use it with caution.

W. C. Ford, ed., *Thomas Jefferson Correspondence, Printed from the Originals in the Collections of Willliam K. Bixby* (Boston, 1916).
Selected from the archives of the Missouri Historical Society, it consists mostly of letters to Jefferson.

Marie Kimball, ed., "Unpublished Correspondence of Mme. de Staël with Thomas Jefferson," *North American Review, 108* (1918), 62–71.
A useful collection of letters from one of Jefferson's few French correspondents who vigorously opposed Napoleon.

Gilbert Chinard, ed., *Les amitiés américaines de madame d'Houdetot d'après sa correspondance inédite avec Benjamin Franklin et Thomas Jefferson* (Paris, 1924).
Through Benjamin Franklin's patronage Mme. d'Houdetot in-

troduced Jefferson to France's literary and philosophical society.
———, ed., *Jefferson et les idéologues d'après sa correspondance inédite avec Destutt de Tracy, Cabanis, J.-B. Say, et Augusté Comte* (Baltimore, 1925).
This volume illuminates the philosophical differences between Jefferson and the *idéologues*.
———, ed., *Trois amitiés françaises de Jefferson d'après sa correspondance inédite avec madame de Brehan, madame de Tessé, et madame de Corny* (Paris, 1927).
The three women, hostesses of Jefferson during his stay in Paris, often embarrassed him with their uncritical affection for America.
———, ed., *The Correspondence of Jefferson and Du Pont de Nemours, with an Introduction on Jefferson and the Physiocrats* (Baltimore, 1931).
Next to Lafayette, Du Pont was Jefferson's closest French friend. He was also an important actor in the negotiations for Louisiana.
———, ed., *Volney et l'Amerique, d'après des documents inédites et sa correspondance avec Jefferson* (Baltimore, 1943).
Volney, a philosopher and scientist, who used his acquaintance with Jefferson in the 1790s to further his studies of America and the policy of the Directory.
Julian P. Boyd and others, eds., *The Papers of Thomas Jefferson* (Princeton, 1950–).
The definitive edition of Jefferson's writings, and a model for current projects on other Founding Fathers.
Lester J. Cappon, ed., *The Adams-Jefferson Letters; The Complete Correspondence between Thomas Jefferson and Abigail and John Adams* (2 vols. Chapel Hill, 1959).
Most valuable for the comments of both men in retirement.

Contemporary Pamphlets

Edmund Randolph, *A Vindication of Mr. Randolph's Resignation* (Philadelphia, 1795).
An explanation of his relations with Fauchet, the French Minister to the United States.
Joseph Fauchet, *A Sketch of the Present State of Our Political Relations with the United States of North-America* (Philadelphia, 1797).
Successor to Genet as Minister to the United States, Fauchet's views cast light on France's impressions of American politics.
James Monroe, *View of the Executive in the Foreign Affairs of the United States Connected with the Mission to the French Republic, 1794–1796* (Philadelphia, 1797).

An apologia for his behavior in France.

Theodore Dwight, *An Oration Spoken at Hartford in the State of Connecticut on the Anniversray of American Independence* (Hartford, 1798).

One of the more effective Federalist tirades against Jefferson as a Francophile.

Abraham Bishop, *Proofs of a Conspiracy, against Christianity, and the Government of the United States* (Hartford, 1802).

A Jeffersonian rebuttal by one of the most articulate Republicans of New England.

George Orr, *The Possesion of Louisiana by the French Considered As It Affected the Interests of Those Nations Most Intimately Concerned viz. Great Britain, America, Spain, and Portugal* (London, 1803).

Friendly to America, the author shows England that Louisiana in French hands constitutes a threat to British possessions as well as to American sovereignty.

Memorial Presented by the Inhabitants of Louisiana to the Congress of the United States (Washington, D.C., 1804).

Complaints of Creoles against American paternalistic government.

Timothy Pickering, *Letter . . . to His Excellency James Sullivan* (Boston, 1808).

A widely publicized letter to the Republican governor of Massachusetts denouncing the embargo.

James Sullivan, *Interesting Correspondence Between His Excellency, Governor Sullivan, and Col. Pickering* (Boston, 1808).

Sullivan's reply to Pickering.

C. M. Talleyrand, *Memoir Concerning the Commercial Relations of the United States with England* (Boston, 1809).

Writing in 1797, Talleyrand realized as an involuntary former resident of the United States that a fundamental pro-British bias in America would always inhibit Franco-American relations.

Robert Walsh, *An Inquiry into the Past and Present Relations of France and the United States* (London, 1811).

A British denunciation of Jefferson's evil influence upon the Madison administration.

François Barbé-Marbois, *The History of Louisiana, Particularly of the Cession of that Colony to the United States of America* (Philadelphia, 1830).

The account of Bonaparte's chief negotiator who was also a friend of the United States.

Gilbert Chinard, ed., *Considerations sur la conduite du gouvernment américain envers la France par L.-G.-Otto* (Princeton, 1945).

A report, written in 1797, denouncing France's policy toward

America on the grounds that it would lead to permanent estrangement.

Official and Semiofficial Documents

The Diplomatic Correspondence of the United States from the Treaty of Peace to the Adoption of the Present (7 vols. Washington, D.C., 1833).
It includes Jefferson's correspondence with Jay during the former's service as minister to France.

W. Lowrie and M. Clark, eds., *American State Papers, Foreign Relations* (6 vols. Washington, D.C., 1832–59).
Badly organized but still useful as a warehouse of diplomatic correspondence.

Annals of the Congress of the United States, 1789–1824 (42 vols. 1834–56).

Collection complète des lois, décrets, ordonnances, règlemens, avis du conseil d'état de 1788 à 1830 (30 vols. Paris, 1835).
The decrees of the successive French governments.

James D. Richardson, ed., *A Compilation of the Messages and Papers of the Presidents, 1789–1902* (10 vols., Washington, D.C., 1899).

Frederick Jackson Turner, "Correspondence of the French Ministers to the United States," *American Historical Association, Annual Report,* 1903 (Washington, D.C., 1904).

W. C. Ford, ed., *Journals of the Continental Congress* (34 vols. Washington, D.C., 1904–36).
Jefferson was a member prior to his appointment to France.

J. A. Robertson, *Louisiana Under Spain, France, and the United States, 1785–1807* (2 vols. Cleveland, 1911).
Among the more useful documents are the reports of Spanish and French officials in New Orleans.

James A. James, ed., "George Rogers Clark Papers, 1771–1784," Virginia Series, 2, *Collections Illinois State Historical Library, 8* (Springfield, 1912).
As governor of Virginia, Jefferson was much concerned with the implications of Clark's expeditions in the Northwest.

E. C. Burnett, ed., *Letters of Members of the Continental Congress* (8 vols. Washington, D.C., 1921–36).

H. R. McIlwaine, ed., *Official Letters of Governors of Virginia* (3 vols. Richmond, 1928).
Jefferson was governor from 1779–81.

David Hunter Miller, *Treaties and Other International Acts of the United States* (6 vols. Washington, D.C., 1931–41).

Bernard Mayo, ed., "Instructions to the British Ministers to the United States, 1791–1812," American Historical Association, *Annual Report*, 1936 (Washington, D.C., 1941).
They contain many comments on Franco-American affairs.

Personal Papers

Gallatin Papers, New York Historical Society
Genet Papers, Library of Congress
Madison Papers, Library of Congress
Monroe Papers, Library of Congress
    New York Public Library
Pickering Papers, Massachusetts Historical Society
John Randolph of Roanoke Papers, Library of Congress
William Short Papers, Library of Congress
Jefferson Papers, Library of Congress
    Massachusetts Historical Society
    University of Virginia

The Library of Congress collection has been the most useful, partly because of its size, and partly because of the great number of letters written to Jefferson which are either unavailable or difficult to locate elsewhere. The libraries of the Massachusetts Historical Society and of the University of Virginia have valuable smaller collections. I have examined in microfilm at the Library of Congress the papers of the Virginia State Library and of the Missouri Historical Society Library. There is nothing of use to my study that may not be found more readily in other collections.

State Papers

National Archives

Department of State Records
    Instructions to United States Ministers to France and Great Britain.
    Despatches from United States Ministers to France and Great Britain.
    These records are of importance during Jefferson's years as Secretary of State and President.

Library of Congress

    France, Archives du ministère des affaires étrangères. Correspondance politique, États-Unis.

Volumes 28 to 62, covering the years 1785 to 1809 are especially useful. They are available in photostats at the Library of Congress. For the most part they contain correspondence between the French ministers to the United States and the foreign ministers in Paris. Occasionally, there is correspondence between the French foreign ministers or even chiefs of state and the American diplomats in Paris.

Great Britain, Public Record Office, Foreign Office Records.
America.
Correspondence of British ministers to the United States with the foreign secretaries. The material in Series 5, vol. 32, dealing with the early part of Jefferson's first administration provides insights into the British image of Jefferson.

Index